The Fundamentals of

Sonic Art & Sound Design

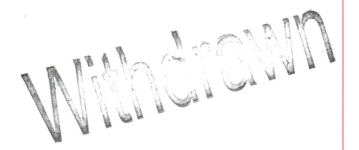

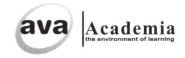

ava | Academia
the environment of learning

An AVA Book
Published by AVA Publishing SA
Rue des Fontenailles 16
Case Postale
1000 Lausanne 6
Switzerland
Tel: +41 786 005 109
Email: enquiries@avabooks.ch

Distributed by Thames & Hudson (ex-North America)
181a High Holborn
London WC1V 7QX
United Kingdom
Tel: +44 20 7845 5000
Fax: +44 20 7845 5055
Email: sales@thameshudson.co.uk
www.thamesandhudson.com

Distributed in the USA & Canada by:
Watson-Guptill Publications
770 Broadway
New York, New York 10003
USA
Fax: +1-646-654-5487
Email: info@watsonguptill.com
www.watsonguptill.com

English Language Support Office
AVA Publishing (UK) Ltd.
Tel: +44 1903 204 455
Email: enquiries@avabooks.co.uk

ISBN 2-940373-49-3 and 978-2-940373-49-9

10 9 8 7 6 5 4 3 2 1

Design by Karen Wilks

Production by AVA Book Production Pte. Ltd., Singapore
Tel: +65 6334 8173
Fax: +65 6259 9830
Email: production@avabooks.com.sg

All reasonable attempts have been made to trace, clear
and credit the copyright holders of the images reproduced
in this book. However, if any credits have been
inadvertently omitted, the publisher will endeavour to
incorporate amendments in future editions.

The Fundamentals of

Sonic Art & Sound Design

Tony Gibbs

Contents

How to get the most out of this book 06
Introduction 08

Origins and Developments 12

Timeline 14
A Historical Perspective 20
A New Form Emerges 30
Sound Design Appears 36

Artists and their Work 40

Art or Music? 42
Vicki Bennett 44
Max Eastley 48
Janek Schaefer 54
Simon Emmerson 62
Knut Aufermann 66

Process and Practice 72

Studio or Laboratory? 74
Designing and Creating Sounds 86
The Computer 94
Interactivity 100

Realisation and Presentation 108

Installations, Environments
and Sculptures 110
Performance 122
Sound Diffusion 132
Exhibiting 140
Media 148

Conclusion 158

Afterword 160
Suggested Reading 162
Suggested Listening 164
Suggested Viewing 166
The Internet 168

Glossary 170
Index 172
Credits 174
Acknowledgements 175

How to get the most out of this book

Chapter titles are shown in the top left-hand corner of each spread.

Pink vertical lines indicate the beginning of each new essay.

Essay titles are shown in the top left-hand corner of each right-hand page.

Chapter numbers are shown in the top right-hand corner of each spread.

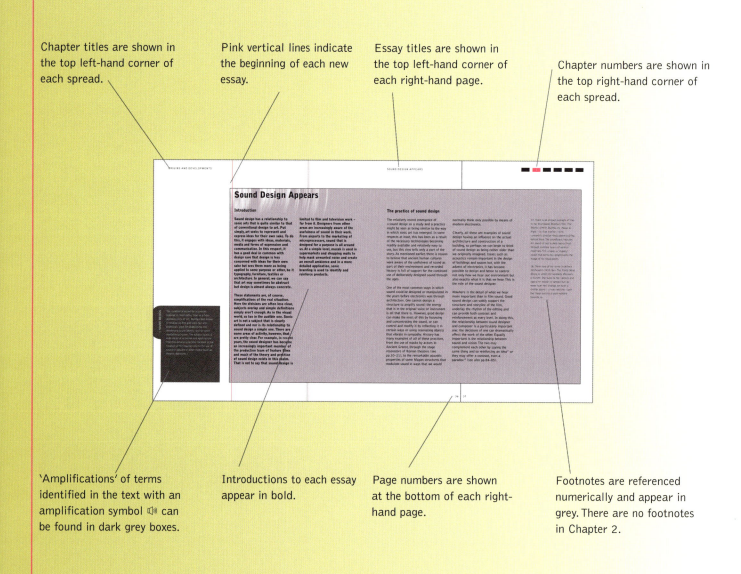

'Amplifications' of terms identified in the text with an amplification symbol 🔊 can be found in dark grey boxes.

Introductions to each essay appear in bold.

Page numbers are shown at the bottom of each right-hand page.

Footnotes are referenced numerically and appear in grey. There are no footnotes in Chapter 2.

Chapter 1.

Discusses the origins and development of the subject. The text is supported by artists' quotations and features a timeline of events important to sonic art and sound design.

Chapter 2.

Features illustrated artist interviews, outlining their biographies and their approach to their work, thus demonstrating the broad scope of the subject.

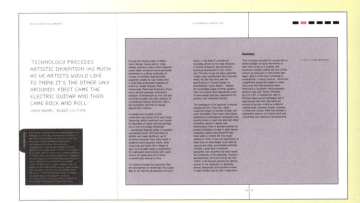

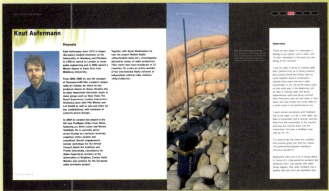

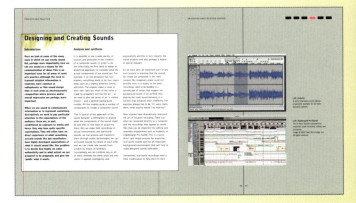

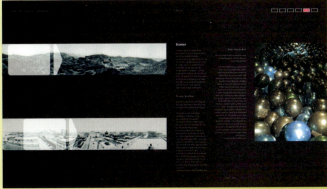

Chapter 3.

Discusses the processes used for making and creating works of sonic art and sound design, and is illustrated by diagrams, screengrabs and equipment, which will familiarise the reader with the available tools.

Chapter 4.

Discusses the processes used to show and display work. Each essay is followed by a selection of photographs of artists' work. Accompanied by extended captions, it is hoped that these displays will inspire the reader in his or her own work.

Introduction

Looking for a definition

Sonic art is a new art form, or rather, forms. As we shall see, it can encompass a wide range of activities, perhaps wider than almost any other art form. It is an unusual case, based upon a medium that has traditionally been regarded as inferior and subservient to other creative or expressive forms. To many composers, sound is simply a means whereby ideas of musical structure and harmony may be expressed: it has little intrinsic value. Likewise to many filmmakers, sound is merely an adjunct to plot and photography and has only a supportive role. However, times have changed and sound now asserts itself as a viable medium in its own right. It can no longer be relegated to a subordinate role, and now demands to be seen as one amongst equals: as a new and distinct medium and potential art form.

Finding the definition of a newly emerged art form is rarely an easy process. There are a number of reasons for this. Firstly, the form itself is often unclear: its advocates usually know where the central focus of the subject lies, but its borders – the points at which it contacts and overlaps other more established forms –

are often far harder to define. Secondly, our new form may encounter resistance to the idea of its own very existence. This can come from a number of sources and for a number of reasons.

Often, the new form originates elsewhere, grows as part of a more established one and, after acquiring an identity of its own, now demands to be recognised independently. The parent genre is often reluctant to let its offspring go its own way, maybe believing that the child is not yet grown up enough to survive the rough-and-tumble of the outside world. Perhaps we should be fair to this point of view; in the case of sonic art, some would say that the child is still a rather difficult adolescent and so the parent's view is understandable even if, from the inside, we believe it to be misguided. Less sympathetic outsiders may take this view further by simply dismissing the fledgling genre as an immature sub-set of something larger and better recognised and by saying that it has no real identity of its own.

Sonic art has encountered all these problems and more besides. The epiphanous moment when the English composer, Trevor Wishart, declared 'Electroacoustic Music is dead – long live Sonic Art'[1] over-simplifies the issue by appearing to suggest that sonic art is simply the offspring of a highly specialised musical activity. In itself, this may be true but his statement tells only a small fraction of the whole story. Sonic art covers a huge range of creative activities, many of which have absolutely nothing to do with music save that, like music, the audience experiences the finished work by hearing it. In some respects it would be perfectly reasonable for our difficult child to round upon its parent (music) and to reverse the argument: all music is sonic art but (as we shall see later) not all sonic art is music! (See Simon Emmerson's comment on p.64.)

These then are just some of the difficulties that we encounter in trying to define what we mean by 'sonic art' or 'sound design'. We can at least make a convenient distinction between these two subjects, however, since we have the existing and well-understood distinctions between visual art and visual design to guide us, and the fact that our work is in a different medium, makes relatively little difference here (see also p.38). To define sonic art in general is, unfortunately, a far less tractable issue. How, for example, can we distinguish between a 'conventional' artwork that happens to make a sound and a work of sound art, and will such a distinction be broadly applicable? I suggested earlier that we might be able to define the centre of our new subject but, since it comes from so many diverse disciplines, it seems to me that sonic art has not one but many centres. So can we give a useful answer at all?

Perhaps the best way to find out about our unruly adolescent is to observe what he does, study the company that he keeps and find out about his background, his parents and siblings. One of the most exciting things about sonic art is the huge size and diversity of the family: from fine art to performance, from film to interactive installations, from poetry to sculpture and, of course, not forgetting music, all these can be part of the multicultural society that is sonic art.

1. Wishart, T. (1996) 'Die elektroakustische Musik ist tot – lang lebe Sonic Art' in *Positionen* (No.29) pp.7–9 (tr. Gisela Nauck).

'THERE IS NO SUCH THING AS AN EMPTY SPACE OR AN EMPTY TIME. THERE IS ALWAYS SOMETHING TO SEE, SOMETHING TO HEAR. IN FACT, TRY AS WE MAY TO MAKE A SILENCE, WE CANNOT.'

JOHN CAGE, 'SILENCE'

What forms can sonic art take?

When we encounter a piece of sonic art, we may find ourselves in front of one of many types of work. Some will be highly interactive and possibly extremely technology-intensive whereas others will be relatively simple and, in a very broad sense, static. However physically static it may be, sound art cannot by its very nature be passive; with rare exceptions it must actively emit sound or at least have sound (which is itself active by definition) as its conceptual basis. Its active emission of sound can, as we shall see later, create problems in the presentation of the work, but it remains an inescapable aspect of the medium and this distinguishes it in some measure from more traditional art forms.

So does it follow that any artwork that has sound as its main 'outcome' will, by definition, be a work of sound art? There are many possible ways in which we can examine this problem and they lead to a variety of conclusions. My personal preference is to take the view that we should define the work by its intentions and by the conceptual thinking that informs it. Thus a work that seeks to communicate with its audience through sound or be informed by ideas that are based upon sound would be a work of sonic art; by contrast, a work that happens to make sounds as a by-product of another activity (as many kinetic works do) or that has no conceptual reference to sound would not.

This is, of course, a very simple definition and has many potential flaws but will hopefully provide us with a useful starting point from which to consider the context in which the presentation of our work takes place. Most importantly, it begins the process of understanding the way in which an audience will experience and comprehend a type of work that may be, in some ways, physically familiar but which is conceptually new and different from other forms.

No single work can hope to provide a comprehensive and detailed approach to a subject that is so diverse and that has so many facets. In this book, we set out to introduce enquiring readers to the subjects of sonic arts and sound design, to show some of the activities that they embrace and, hopefully, to kindle an interest in these new and exciting areas.

Unlike many academic (and even artistic) subjects, there is no fixed 'syllabus' for our work. It will become apparent to readers that, while the centre of our subject is clear, its edges are less well defined: sonic art spills over into fine art, music, performance, ecology and many other areas. This means that what you have in your hands is not a textbook in the conventional sense; rather it could be thought of as a catalogue of ideas or a menu of possibilities. Above all, it is an invitation to enter and become part of a new and exciting world – one that *you* can help to define.

1

Origins and Developments

The relationship between art and technology is a fascinating and many-sided one. For some, the technology merely provides the tools with which to create the art while, for others, it suggests new possibilities and even provides the fundamental inspiration that drives and informs the entire creative process. Most works of sonic art use technologies to a greater or lesser extent although, as we shall see, the widely held presumption that this whole art form is critically dependent upon high technology (and computers in particular) is far from being universally true. What is certain, however, is that the evolution of sonic art as a distinct form has been very closely linked to the development of audio technologies and, in the following section, we will begin to explore this evolving relationship.

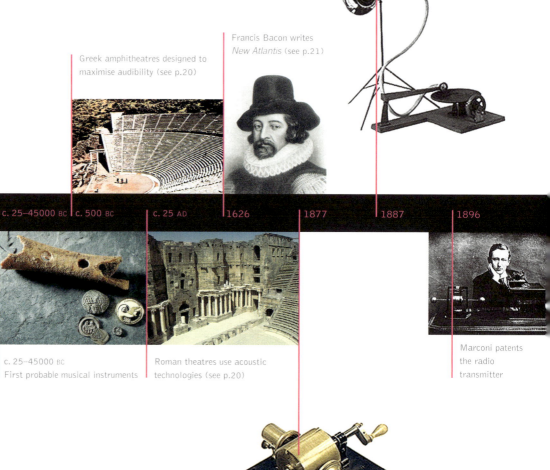

Disk recording invented by
Emile Berliner

Francis Bacon writes
New Atlantis (see p.21)

Greek amphitheatres designed to
maximise audibility (see p.20)

Timeline

| c. 25–45000 BC | c. 500 BC | c. 25 AD | 1626 | 1877 | 1887 | 1896 |

c. 25–45000 BC
First probable musical instruments

Roman theatres use acoustic
technologies (see p.20)

Marconi patents
the radio
transmitter

The Edison Phonograph – the first
recording system (see page 24)

Valdemar Poulsen invents the 'Telegraphone' – the first magnetic recorder

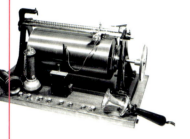

Lev Termen (Leo Theremin) develops the Theremin

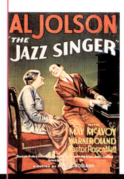

Talking pictures – premiere of *The Jazz Singer* (see p.25)

Russolo writes the *Art of Noises* manifesto (see pp.22–23)

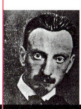

First commercial radio station – KDKA in Pittsburgh USA (see p.25)

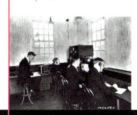

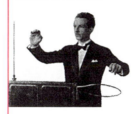

Invention of the jukebox

1898	1906	1913	1914	1920	1925	1927	1931	1933

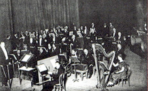

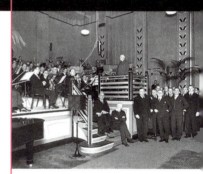

First concert of *Intonarumori* in Milan (see p.23)

Electrically recorded disks appear

Abbey Road Studios open

The Edison Multiphone – the forerunner of the jukebox

Robert Beyer and Werner Meyer-Eppler propose 'electronic music'

The LP record is marketed by Columbia

Pierre Henry and Pierre Schaeffer found the 'Groupe de Recherche de Musique Concrète' (see p.26)

Premiere of John Cage's *4'33"* given by David Tudor (see p.34)

Karlheinz Stockhausen composes *Kontakte*

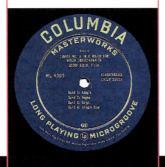

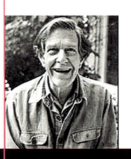

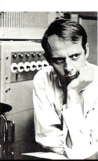

1935   1947   1948   1949   1951   1952   1958   1959

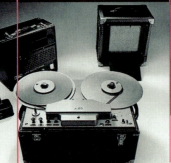

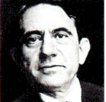

West Deutsche Rundfunk opens electronic music studio in Cologne

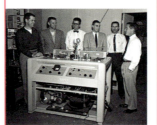

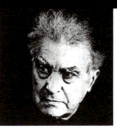

Pierre Schaeffer creates early 'Musique Concrète' work, *Étude aux chemins de fer* (see p.26)

Edgard Varèse's *Poeme Électronique* multimedia work at Brussels World Fair (see pp. 30–31)

The stereo record is marketed

AEG 'Magnetophon' – the first practical tape recorder premiered at Berlin Radio Fair (see p.25)

The video recorder is developed by Ampex

Robert Moog develops the Moog synthesiser

'Cybernetic Serendipity' exhibition brings computer art to the UK public

The laserdisk is announced by Sony

The Beatles release *Revolver*

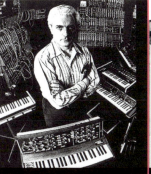

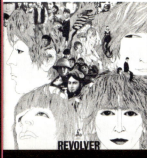

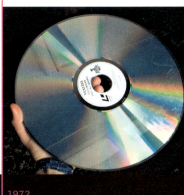

| 1963 | 1964 | 1965 | 1966 | 1967 | 1968 | 1969 | 1972 |

Steve Reich composes tape works *Come Out* and *It's Gonna Rain* (see p.32)

The audio cassette is announced by Philips

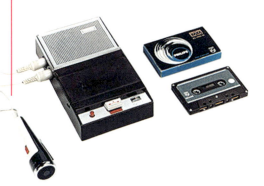

The Beatles release *Sgt Pepper's Lonely Hearts Club Band*

John Cage creates *HPSCHD,* a five-hour multimedia work

French president Georges Pompidou initiates IRCAM under the direction of Pierre Boulez

VHS/Betamax video format wars

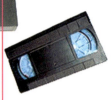

IBM launches the personal computer

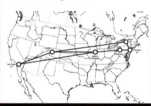

NSFNet (immediate precursor of
the Internet) goes live

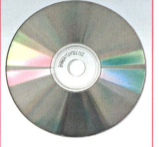

Sonic Arts Network formed

SonicArtsNetwork

| 1975 | 1975/6 | 1979 | 1981 | 1982 | 1983 | 1984 | 1989 |

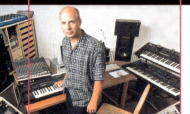

Brian Eno announces ambient
music (see p.39)

The Fairlight CMI is unveiled by
Peter Vogel and Kim Ryrie

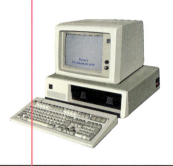

Philips introduces the compact disk

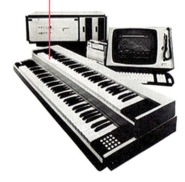

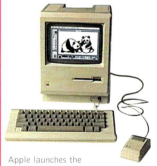

Apple launches the
Macintosh computer

The DVD appears

Trevor Wishart declares sonic art
as a distinct form (see p.9)

Curated by David Toop, 'Sonic Boom'
exhibition brings sound art to the
London public

Jem Finer's sonic art work
Longplayer begins its 1,000-year run
(see pp.111–115)

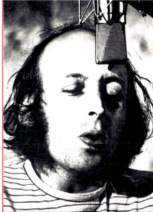

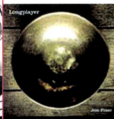

| 1992 | 1996 | 1998 | 2000 | 2001 |

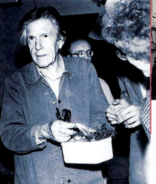

The BBC closes the Radiophonic
Workshop (opened in 1958)

Apple launches the iPod

Death of John Cage (b.1912)

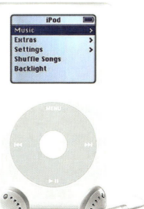

A Historical Perspective

Introduction

No one knows with any certainty when man became consciously aware of the significance of sound and, more importantly, of the possibility of controlling and using it for other than purely practical purposes. The cupping of the hand behind the ear to focus a distant sound is a gesture so old as to be more-or-less instinctive. It is only a small step from this idea to that of placing the hands in a horn-like form in front of the mouth in order to help project the voice. Here, for the first time, we see a deliberate attempt to influence the sounds that we make and hear. In these instances, the purpose is simple vocal communication but there is substantial evidence to suggest that ancient man used technology to control sound and that he did so for quite complex purposes. We can certainly assume that cultures much older than ours were aware of at least some of the ways in which they could control sound. Indeed, we can still find long-established and specialised forms of vocal communication in remote and mountainous regions.[1]

Sound without electricity

Round about the time of the last Ice Age, the first recognisable musical instruments started to appear and people began to make use of the acoustic properties of particular spaces and places. Early instruments seem to have been predominantly based upon natural objects such as conch shells and hollow bones. Several researchers[2] have also noted that cave paintings are often to be found in locations where the local acoustics have unusual qualities, and this has led to speculation that these places may have been venues for early forms of multimedia events.[3] Howard Rheingold[4] goes further and suggests that the combination of cave paintings, unusual acoustics, costume and other practices such as fasting, sleep deprivation, etc. may have been combined to create a low-technology form of virtual reality that could be used as part of rituals, initiation rites and so forth. Whether or not these practices could be considered as 'art' is debatable, but we may reasonably think of them as applied art at least and possibly, therefore, a form of design. The question to be considered here is the extent to which our ancestors were aware of how a particular acoustic quality was created and how it could be manipulated. History, unfortunately, is silent on this issue and we must look to later cultures before we begin to see strong evidence of deliberate design of acoustics and, hence, of sound.

We don't have far to look: the Ancient Greeks were undoubtedly well aware of how to control acoustics and the almost miraculous sonic qualities of their open air theatres testify to their skills. Architecture, however, was by no means the whole story: the Greeks (and later the Romans) also made extensive use of masks that contained horn-like structures or resonating cavities that served to reinforce and project the voice.

The Romans took Greek sound technologies a stage further and provided quite extensive sound systems in many of their theatres. These, of course, were nothing like the sound systems that we would recognise today since even the best Roman technology could not amplify a sound. What it could do, however, was to make the most of the volume available by using resonators (large vases partially filled with water) or by placing actors in front of a membrane that was tightly stretched over a recess in the back wall of the stage. By the first century BC these, and other sound-controlling procedures, were well-established parts of theatre design by architects such as Marcus Vitruvius Pollo. According to Bruce Smith '...a Vitruvian theatre could be played by actors as if it were a musical instrument.'[5] What we see here is the first clear evidence of deliberate sound design in the theatre.

Sound design remained the property of architects for almost the whole of the following millennium. There were some notable exceptions, however, such as the use of surround sound in the composition of works by (amongst others) Monteverdi. Here, composers would write music that was designed to be performed in particular churches with musicians and singers placed, not on stage, but in various locations around the building. Not only did this lend a spatial element to the performance but it also allowed for different musical parts to be accompanied by more or less reverberation: choices more normally exercised in our times by record producers and sound engineers (see also pp.78–79). This is not to suggest, however, that there was a lack of awareness of the potential of sound as an expressive medium in its own right, but rather, the technologies that were needed to allow it to develop simply did not yet exist. For example, in his speculative but prescient 1626 work *New Atlantis*,[6] the English philosopher Francis Bacon describes facilities that not only resemble a modern recording studio but also anticipate the type of work undertaken in the most advanced computer graphics houses:

We have also soundhouses, where we practise and demonstrate all sounds and their generation. We have harmony which you have not of quarter sounds and lesser slides of sounds. Divers instruments of music likewise to you unknown, some sweeter than any you have; with bells and rings that are dainty and sweet.

We represent small sounds as great and deep, likewise great sounds extenuate and sharp; we make divers tremblings and warblings of sounds, which in their original are entire. We represent and imitate all articulate sounds and letters, and the voices and notes of beasts and birds.

We have certain helps which, set to ear, do further the hearing greatly; we have also divers strange and artificial echoes, reflecting the voice many times, and, as it were, tossing it; and some that give back the voice louder than it came, some shriller and some deeper; yea, some rendering the voice, differing in the letters or articulate sound from that they receive. We have all means to convey sounds in trunks and pipes, in strange lines and distances.

1. For example the Silbo language of the Canaries uses whistling to communicate over long distances in these mountainous islands.

2. Devereux, P. (2003) *Stone Age Soundtracks*. London: Vega (Chrysalis).
Waller, Steven J., *Rock Art Acoustics* website <www.geocities.com/cape canaveral/9461/> accessed 05/02/06.

3. *New Scientist* (28 Nov 1992) quoted in Toop, D. (1995) *Ocean of Sound*. London: Serpent's Tail.

4. Rheingold, H. (1991) *Virtual Reality*. London: Penguin.

5. Smith, B.R. (1999) *The Acoustic World of Early Modern England*. Chicago, IL: University of Chicago Press.

6. Bacon, F. (1626) *New Atlantis*.

EVERY MANIFESTATION OF OUR LIFE IS ACCOMPANIED BY NOISE. THE NOISE, THEREFORE, IS FAMILIAR TO OUR EAR, AND HAS THE POWER TO CONJURE UP LIFE ITSELF. SOUND, ALIEN TO OUR LIFE, ALWAYS MUSICAL AND A THING UNTO ITSELF, AN OCCASIONAL BUT UNNECESSARY ELEMENT, HAS BECOME TO OUR EARS WHAT AN OVERFAMILIAR FACE IS TO OUR EYES.

NOISE, HOWEVER, REACHING US IN A CONFUSED AND IRREGULAR WAY FROM THE IRREGULAR CONFUSION OF OUR LIFE, NEVER ENTIRELY REVEALS ITSELF TO US, AND KEEPS INNUMERABLE SURPRISES IN RESERVE. WE ARE THEREFORE CERTAIN THAT BY SELECTING, COORDINATING AND DOMINATING ALL NOISES WE WILL ENRICH MEN WITH A NEW AND UNEXPECTED SENSUAL PLEASURE.

ALTHOUGH IT IS CHARACTERISTIC OF NOISE TO RECALL US BRUTALLY TO REAL LIFE, THE ART OF NOISE MUST NOT LIMIT ITSELF TO IMITATIVE REPRODUCTION. IT WILL ACHIEVE ITS MOST EMOTIVE POWER IN THE ACOUSTIC ENJOYMENT, IN ITS OWN RIGHT, THAT THE ARTIST'S INSPIRATION WILL EXTRACT FROM COMBINED NOISES.

LUIGI RUSSOLO, THE 'ART OF NOISES' MANIFESTO, 1913

The Art of Noises

Perhaps one of the most significant developments in sound art and design used relatively simple mechanical technologies: the importance, however, was not so much the technology as the ideas that it expressed. The work of the Futurists, an Italian art movement of the early 1900s, included one of the most famous documents in sonic art: the *Art of Noises*[7] manifesto of 1913.

Written in the form of a letter from the painter Luigi Russolo to the composer Francesco Pratella, it puts forward the idea that there should be no barriers (or even distinctions) between sounds that have musical or instrumental origins and those that come from the street, from industry or even from warfare. Russolo suggests that all these sound sources should be incorporated into the creation of a new form of music. Interestingly, Russolo does not suggest a new form of art that is based upon sound: what he proposes is simply an extension of existing practices in music (this is an argument that continues to the present day). Sonic art, it seems, is still some way in the future but at least the idea of using non-musical sounds in art has begun to be established and this was acknowledged many years later in the name of one of the first pop bands of the 1980s to make extensive use of sampling technology: Trevor Horn's The Art of Noise.[8]

In 1913, however, there was no usable technology that would allow the incorporation of real-world sounds into musical performances – clearly a gramophone would be inaudible over the sound of an orchestra – so Russolo created a series of machines known as *Intonarumori* or Noise Intoners,[9] each dedicated to the production of particular types of noises and being given splendidly expressive Italian names such as *Ululator* – the howler, *Crepitatori* – the cracker and *Stropicciatore* – the rubber. These instruments saw limited service in a number of concerts but, sadly, none have survived in their original form.

The *Intonarumori* were revolutionary only in the sense that they, and the *Art of Noises* manifesto, argued the case for sound in the broadest sense to be considered in the way normally reserved for music and composers, instruments and the performers that create it.

They were not themselves particularly groundbreaking technologies that opened up new creative possibilities, but they did argue the case for sound to be something considered in its own right and, by so doing, laid the foundation for what later became the disciplines of sonic art and sound design.

7. See opposite.

8. English record producer Trevor Horn created The Art of Noise (sic) as part of his own record label, ZTT, itself an allusion to another Futurist work, *Bombardamento*, a Futurist sound poem of 1914 by Filippo Tommaso Marinetti, in which the phrase 'Zang Tumb Tumb' supposedly represented the sounds of a battle that took place at Adrianopolis in 1912.

9. Excellent audio examples of these instruments can be found at <www.thereminvox.com/filemanager/list/12/> accessed 04/02/06.

'INDEED, ONE COULD SAY THAT BY THE LATE 1980S THE AGE OF COMPUTER MUSIC WAS OVER BECAUSE EVERYTHING WAS COMPUTER MUSIC.'

JOEL CHADABE, 'ELECTRIC SOUND'

RADIOPHONICS

Originally defined as sound designed specifically for radio broadcasting, the term has now taken on a broader range of meanings. These include the general area of acousmatics (sound that is heard without reference to its visual origin), narrative (such as radio drama) and some overlapping aspects of soundscape work. Pioneered (in terms of public awareness) in the early 1960s by the BBC Radiophonic Workshop in London, this area now stretches significantly beyond broadcasting to include some forms of electroacoustic work, especially those with a narrative element.

The impact of electronics

Serious sound design and, subsequently, sonic art had to await the advent of recording and, more particularly, of electronics following the First World War. The recording process itself is widely acknowledged to have been invented in 1877 by Thomas Edison. However, there is some evidence for earlier dates including a charming – if improbable – tale told by the late Hugh Davies: the door of a Chinese temple had a stylus attached to it which, as the door closed, tracked along a groove in the floor. This groove apparently carried a recording which politely thanked the visitor for closing the door![10]

Early 'acoustic' recording systems were functional but offered only limited scope as creative tools: they could record and play back but, apart from speeding up and slowing down the sound, they could do very little else. The advent of electronics transformed this situation. The microphone replaced the mechanical horn and recordings were now cut electrically. This immediately opened up a huge range of possibilities: the outputs of multiple microphones could be combined, the signals that they created could be processed in all manner of ways and even simple multi-tracking became possible. These technologies joined with the advent of the radio station (KDKA in Pittsburgh USA in 1920) and talking pictures (*The Jazz Singer* in 1927) and, between them, provided the tools for an explosion of creative possibilities in sound art and design. The ultimate tool, however, was the tape recorder, which made its public debut at the Berlin Radio Fair in 1935. Until the widespread adoption of the computer as a means of recording and transforming sound in the latter years of the twentieth century, this remained the primary resource for creative activities in sound.

However, not all sonic art or sound design activities required the tape recorder. An early example of radiophonic art was the 1938 radio dramatisation of H.G. Wells' book *The War of the Worlds*. This caused widespread panic throughout the United States as a result of its remarkable realism. Material created in a small radio studio was carefully crafted to create the illusion of live location reporting of an alien invasion. The technologies used were simple by modern standards but the

impact was dramatic and the widespread assumption that what was heard was 'real' rather than a studio production, only served to demonstrate the relationship between radio and its audience. In doing this, it established at least one important component of the foundations of ⁤radiophonics: the believability of radio.

The director of this project, Orson Welles, was also a film director and, unusually for the time, made creative use of sound in his movies. Notably, in his 1941 film *Citizen Kane*, he employs a hollow, echoing acoustic in a scene where the main character bemoans the emptiness of his world and, elsewhere, uses several layers of sound simultaneously. Welles continued to develop this interest in film sound in later works such as *The Magnificent Ambersons*. Although limited from the perspective of contemporary, effects-laden productions, we see here the beginnings of specifically and creatively designed film sound; a significant step forward from simple recording of dialogue, sound effects and music that had been the norm in film production.

10. Davies, H. (1996) 'A History of sampling', in *Organised Sound*, Vol.1.

Electroacoustic music

Elsewhere, other artists and composers were undertaking sound-based work. In France, Pierre Schaeffer, a radio engineer, began to experiment with recording as a way of treating sounds and assembling them into new forms. Initially, despite their limitations, Schaeffer used disk recorders and players in his work – a clear precursor of the modern experimental DJ techniques used by artists such as Janek Schaefer, Christian Marclay and others. These experiments led to a classic work, *Étude aux chemins de fer*, which took location recordings of trains and treated and combined them into a work that, although clearly composed, was by no means music in the conventional sense. Schaeffer went on to work with tape recorders, including specially built machines such as the 'Phonogene', which allowed tape recordings to be played using a keyboard. This was one of the several ancestors of the modern sampler and, for the first time, allowed non-musical sound sources to be treated in the same way as conventional instruments. However, treating real-world sounds as if they were musical instruments was by no means the only, or indeed the most interesting, approach to working with abstract sound.[11]

The specialised machinery developed by Schaeffer and others for handling 'real' sounds was paralleled by developments in the creation of sound by electronic means – what we now refer to as sound synthesis. The early works of composers such as Karlheinz Stockhausen used equipment from electronics laboratories to generate and transform sounds from scratch and to assemble them into finished compositions. This approach was known as electronic music.

At this time (the 1950s and early 1960s), synthesisers had yet to be invented and so anyone wanting to work with electronic sounds had to build their own equipment. One of the most notable such inventors was Raymond Scott. A composer who specialised in music for advertising, Scott quickly spotted the ear-catching commercial potential of electronically generated sound and, using the extraordinary variety of equipment that he created through his company, Manhattan Research, became widely known for original and creative sound design for radio and television advertising.[12]

An interesting hybrid between the work of Scott and more abstract forms came in the activities of the BBC Radiophonic Workshop. This facility, opened in 1958, was initially developed to meet the demands of makers of radio dramas for special effects but became a substantial organisation in its own right, creating a wide range of specialised musical and other material including, in 1963, the famous theme from the television series *Doctor Who* (created by Delia Derbyshire and Ron Grainer) and a radio version of Douglas Adams' work *The Hitchhiker's Guide to the Galaxy* in 1978. The Radiophonic Workshop contributed very substantially to the development of an experimental tradition in electroacoustic music in the UK and, up until its closure in 1998, was a significant focus for composers and engineers and other practitioners. It is also important to note that, insofar as much of the work of the Radiophonic Workshop was commissioned to be included in radio and television programmes, it could quite appropriately be regarded (in many cases, at least) as being more sound design than sound art.

The appearance of the commercial synthesiser in the mid-1960s provided a substantial catalyst for new developments. The synthesiser came to public awareness

11. Interestingly, Schaeffer called his work 'Musique Concrète' meaning that the 'music' was to be derived from 'concrete' (i.e. real) sources rather than 'Musique Abstraite' which was his term for the conventional process of composition followed by performance and (possibly) recording.

12. Excellent audio examples of Raymond Scott's work can be found at <www.raymondscott.com> and on the double CD set *Manhattan Research Inc.*

'WHAT I LIKE ABOUT THE UNTIDY MESS OF COMMUNICATIONS PRODUCED BY THE NEW TECHNOLOGIES IS THAT NOTHING IS PRESCRIBED, NOTHING IS COMPLETE AND ABOVE ALL THERE IS NO PRETENCE. EVERYTHING IS WILD, EXPERIMENTAL, PRECARIOUS...'
MICHEL JAFFRENNOU, 'DIGITAL AND VIDEO ART'

ELECTRONIC MUSIC

Later referred to as 'electroacoustic music'. Based upon the theoretical researches of Robert Beyer, Herbert Eimert, Werner Meyer-Eppler and others and originating in the works of (amongst others) Pierre Schaeffer and Karlheinz Stockhausen, this subject includes the composition and realisation of musical works using sound sources that are wholly or partly electronic in origin and, increasingly, sounds derived from 'real world' sources that are subsequently treated by a range of electronic processes. Originally based around the use of synthesisers (and their forerunners) and tape recorders, the work is increasingly undertaken using the digital processes available in modern computer systems. Some of these are highly sophisticated and often experimental procedures such as phase vocoding, granulation and convolution. Technical sophistication is often paralleled by advanced compositional forms and procedures including algorithmic and chance processes as well as by more traditional approaches such as serialism. It is the subject of extensive and detailed scholarship and is predominantly (although by no means exclusively) carried out under the aegis of academic institutions.

'TECHNOLOGY PRECEDES ARTISTIC INVENTION (AS MUCH AS WE ARTISTS WOULD LIKE TO THINK IT'S THE OTHER WAY AROUND!). FIRST CAME THE ELECTRIC GUITAR AND THEN CAME ROCK AND ROLL.'

JOHN ADAMS, 'AUDIO CULTURE'

SOUNDSCAPING

A soundscape can be said to be the audible equivalent of a landscape. Put simply, it is a representation of a place or environment through what can be heard rather than what can be seen. Like their photographic equivalents, soundscapes can be realistic and so be directly representational or they can use modifications of (and additions to) the original sounds to create a more subjective sound picture, rather like using a lens to change perspective or a filter to alter colour. Closely related to some aspects of acoustic ecology, the concept of the soundscape emerged in the late 1960s in the form of the World Soundscape Project. Led by R. Murray Schafer and Barry Truax, this research group first documented their own locality through audio recordings in *The Vancouver Soundscape* (1973) and went on to make extensive documentary recordings in Canada and Europe. Soundscaping is not only a documentary medium but is also used as a compositional form by practitioners such as Hildegard Westerkamp.

through the musical work of Walter (later Wendy) Carlos and his 1968 release *Switched-on Bach*, which featured classic Bach orchestral works performed exclusively on a Moog synthesiser. A number of similarly inspired works appeared, notably by Isao Tomita who created lush synthesised renditions of works by Claude Debussy, Holst, Mussorgsky, Ravel and Stravinsky. These works and the generally enthusiastic adoption of synthesisers by rock and pop musicians brought new sonic textures to conventional musical forms but, with a few exceptions, did little to expand beyond their confines.

A conspicuous exception to this convention was Carlos' 1972 work *Sonic Seasonings*, which could only very loosely be described as 'music' and was perhaps one of the first widely distributed soundscape-inspired works. It exploited synthesised sound, field recordings of wildlife and made significant use of technical processes more often found in academic electroacoustic works. *Sonic Seasonings* and works like it began to open up a broader range of possibilities for exploration and creation with sound and by no means were all of these conventionally musical in form.

It is hard to escape the conclusion that the development of technology had a good deal to do with the development of sound works. In the field of commercial recording, driven by the huge revenues of record companies and performers, technical development in the 1960s and '70s was, to say the least, explosive. Studios were transformed into resources, which, for the first time, met the specification of 'Sound Houses' as described by Francis Bacon.[13] Despite the remarkable power of these systems, their cost placed them beyond the reach of most people and they maintained this position until relatively recently.

The emergence of the personal computer changed all this. From the 1980s, computers began to become smaller and more affordable. From room-sized giants operated by multinational companies, they quickly shrank in both size and cost while increasing rapidly in power and performance. Soon it became possible for private individuals to have in their homes computers vastly more powerful than those used to control the first moon landing in 1969. It was not long before at least some of these began to be used for musical and other sound-based activities. Initially, a good deal of external equipment was required and many found the complexity of this daunting. However, developments continued and by the mid-1990s it had become possible for almost anyone to use computers to generate, record, manipulate and transform sound in ways limited only by their imagination.

Summary

Thus it became possible for anyone with a modest budget to equip themselves to work with sound as a creative and expressive medium and by the turn of the century an explosion of such works had begun. Much of this work remained in conventional – mainly musical – forms but a significant proportion began to move into areas that had previously been restricted to 'academic' electroacoustic practice (see also 'Sound Diffusion' pp.132–139). A substantial shift in thinking about sound had begun and it was through this shift that sonic art started to become visible as a distinct creative area. However, largely unknown to these new artists, there was already a substantial amount of creative work and scholarship just waiting to be discovered.

13. Bacon, F. (1626) *New Atlantis.*

A New Form Emerges

Introduction

As we have seen, in the post-war period technical possibilities began to develop at a dramatic rate and so did the thinking of practitioners of sonic art and sound design. These titles were not in use at the time: most creators of this type of work were still referred to as composers, engineers or editors and their work was discussed in appropriate terms. This is perhaps not surprising since many of them came from traditional musical backgrounds and had only opted to work in new and developing areas after a 'conventional' training. It follows that a good deal of the work that was created quite rightly belongs under the title of 'music'. Equally, however, an increasing amount of work simply did not fit in this category and artists sometimes found themselves in an increasingly problematic situation as a result.

Edgard Varèse

One notable example was the work created by French composer Edgard Varèse for the 1958 Brussels Expo (the Brussels Universal Exhibition – the first post-war World Fair, taking the theme 'A World View – A New Humanism'). His *Poeme Électronique* was, in many respects, something that we would regard nowadays as an installation work or indeed a work of sonic art rather than a piece of music. It used up to 425 loudspeakers distributed around the Le Corbusier-designed Phillips Pavilion and also included film and slide projections and lighting effects. The sounds were both concrete and electronic in origin and were processed using a range of techniques, many of them developed from the work of Pierre Schaeffer. Critics usually discuss this work in musical terms but this is clearly only part of the story since Varèse himself expressed at least as strong an interest in sound itself as he did in music and, in any event, sound was just one component amongst several that made up the work as a whole.

'IT CONSISTED OF MOVING COLOURED LIGHTS, IMAGES PROJECTED ON THE WALLS OF THE PAVILION, AND MUSIC. THE MUSIC WAS DISTRIBUTED BY 425 LOUDSPEAKERS; THERE WERE TWENTY AMPLIFIER COMBINATIONS. IT WAS RECORDED ON A THREE-TRACK MAGNETIC TAPE THAT COULD BE VARIED IN INTENSITY AND QUALITY. THE LOUDSPEAKERS WERE MOUNTED IN GROUPS AND IN WHAT IS CALLED 'SOUND ROUTES' TO ACHIEVE VARIOUS EFFECTS SUCH AS THAT OF THE MUSIC RUNNING AROUND THE PAVILION, AS WELL AS COMING FROM DIFFERENT DIRECTIONS, REVERBERATIONS ETC. FOR THE FIRST TIME, I HEARD MY MUSIC LITERALLY PROJECTED INTO SPACE.'
EDGARD VARÈSE, DESCRIBING 'POEME ÉLECTRONIQUE'

Developments in music and art

Steve Reich is normally regarded as a composer who specialises in the musical form known as 'minimalism'. This relies, in part, on repetition and is now a well-established style. Some of Reich's early works, however, are clearly not music in the conventional sense. His tape pieces *Come Out* (1966) and *It's Gonna Rain* (1965) use the spoken word exclusively. They are also entirely dependent upon a technical process: the slightly out-of-sync repeating of two similar tape loops and their interaction. Apart from the repetition – which creates a rhythmic structure – these works can hardly be regarded as being musical in any meaningful sense. We hear the words repeated over and over and we hear the subtle ways in which they interact with each other and how these interactions change. We also experience the odd feeling that when a word is repeated many times it slowly loses any meaning. After a few minutes, we have no sense that rain is imminent: instead we're hearing a shifting pattern of sounds that happens to be made from words. Should we regard this as a very extended form of music or, since it depends upon a technical process, is it something else altogether? The problem here is that Reich is traditionally regarded as being a composer. Composers are expected by most people to compose music and, unless they take up painting or

sculpture as a hobby, composers are not expected to create art.

A number of composers had by now expanded the scope of their work beyond the accepted boundaries of composition and performance and some of their work could clearly no longer be simply described as 'music' in the conventional sense. Nor could much of it be covered by the rather cautious term ◁»'experimental music'. One of the main problems was that much of this new work had crossed into other subject areas that were informed by different theories and traditions. Practitioners who were normally thought of as being fine artists encountered much the same problem. However, this group had something of an advantage since, at this time, contemporary art as a whole was in a state of flux and new forms emerged almost daily.

For these artists and their public, the idea of the work taking a new form was far more acceptable than was the case for composers who found themselves in a similar situation. It seems that 'art' thinking was, in some respects, more flexible and accommodating than 'music' thinking and was prepared to accept the idea that art could be made from (or with) sound that stepped outside the

conventions of music. The musical 'establishment' was, it seems, rather less flexible in this respect and tended to insist that a work be described in musical, rather than abstract terms, or those used within art in general. This is not to suggest that the art establishment welcomed our fledgling subject as enthusiastically as its musical opposite number had rejected it. One of the issues for many people was the use of technologies and processes that could not be undertaken without them. We have only to consider the techniques of painting and sculpture to realise that the idea that art could be created through the means of technology was not new. However, the nature of some of the technologies that were beginning to be used was wholly different to what had gone before and, for many people, something about this situation simply did not sit comfortably.

In the early 1960s, a number of artists became interested in 'high' technology: sound and video recording systems. This was coupled with the development of a number of new approaches to art, including the idea of interaction between the viewer and the work. Clearly, when one looks at a painting and it stimulates a response, there is a degree of interaction but this process does not affect the picture itself so we have only a very limited form of interactivity. The idea that the work could respond to and even be controlled by the viewer was a radical one and opened up questions regarding the relationships between artist, artwork and audience. Similarly, art movements such as the UK group Fluxus began to explore the idea of performance as art. Add to this the emergence of readily available technologies and a time of turbulent social change and new forms and practices in art became more-or-less inevitable.

Throughout this period, art experimented with film, video and sound – indeed any medium that became available. The work of established artists such as Nam June Paik crossed over many technologies and forms of practice but still remained fairly and squarely under the overall heading of 'art'. Even when the technological aspects of the work became broadly accepted, the work retained all the traditional qualities of art: the theories that informed it, the places in which it was exhibited, the way in which critics regarded it and so on were all those that had been associated with traditional forms. Add to this the idea that we could be looking at a wholly new art form and it becomes easy to understand why sonic art has had such a difficult birth and why it still struggles to be truly independent and widely accepted.

'I USE TECHNOLOGY IN ORDER TO HATE IT MORE PROPERLY. I MAKE TECHNOLOGY LOOK RIDICULOUS.'

NAM JUNE PAIK, 'DIGITAL AND VIDEO ART'

EXPERIMENTAL MUSIC

Experimental music is almost impossible to define since what is experimental today can become commonplace tomorrow. For example, in 1975, Brian Eno created a highly experimental work called *Discreet Music* (see p.39 and pp.78–79). This became the basis for what is now known as ambient music and, in so doing, ceased to be regarded as experimental. Similarly, in the 1960s, Steve Reich created works (such as *Come Out* and *It's Gonna Rain*) using looped sounds – much current popular electronic music is now substantially based upon looped material. Experimental music is perhaps more usefully defined as an approach to composition and performance that uses unconventional techniques. These may take the form of aleatory processes, in which decisions normally taken by the composer are taken by other means such as the laws of mathematical chance or algorithmic processes.

CHANCE

Chance, as we might use the word, is perhaps a somewhat misleading term since its application to both sonic and visual arts can lead to highly structured and deterministic results. Chance music is otherwise known as aleatory music and may use a range of processes to determine aspects of structure and content that are normally defined directly by the composer. Decisions and choices may be made by mathematical, graphical or statistical methods (amongst others) and, in some instances, may involve the use of computer systems to define structure and content from a set of given rules or algorithms. Notable users of chance have included John Cage, Pierre Boulez and Iannis Xenakis.

John Cage

One of the figures that looms largest in the evolution of sonic art is that of John Cage. Following studies with composer Arnold Schoenberg and artist Marcel Duchamp, it was perhaps inevitable that his work would follow an unconventional path. Cage's art often used chance and ranged freely across many media. He composed music (conventional and otherwise), collaborated with choreographer Merce Cunningham, wrote, painted and created early multimedia events such as *Variations V* (1965) in which a sound system devised by Cage and sound engineer Billy Klüver interacted with dancers and visual components, including films and video images by Nam June Paik. A significant recognition of the amazingly diverse nature of his work came in the form of the award in 1986 of a very unusual title – Doctor of All the Arts – by the California Institute of Arts.

Despite the extraordinary breadth of his works, Cage remained devoted to sound in all its aspects from his controversial composition *4' 33"* (1952) in which a 'silence' lasting four minutes and 33 seconds is created (or 'performed') to works for multiple tape recorders (*Williams Mix* – 1952/3)[14] and his radical view that the artist should allow sounds to speak for themselves.[15] Despite the fact that he continued to refer to much of his work as being 'music', by such works and statements, Cage effectively created the idea that sound by itself could communicate and, perhaps more importantly (for us at least), that it could be the basis for a distinct art form. These statements are easily made but Cage's work did much to substantiate them and force sceptics to take the idea seriously: such works included his early *Sonatas and Interludes for Prepared Piano* (1946–48). In these works, Cage insists that we pay at least as much attention to sound itself as to more conventionally musical considerations like harmony or melody. Although always willing to use technology,[16] on this occasion Cage reverts to a far simpler approach, transforming the sound of that most quintessentially 'musical' of instruments – the piano. He achieves this by inserting objects (washers, screws, pieces of rubber etc.) at precise positions between the strings of the piano, removing much of the 'piano-ness' from the instrument and turning it into something altogether different: an unknown instrument whose interest lies at least as much in its unusual sound as in the music that it plays. Perhaps this is a subtle shift in emphasis but equally one that allows us to focus upon music as something that relies upon sound for its expression rather than the other way round.

Of course, no single individual is ever wholly responsible for the emergence of a new art form and it would be quite wrong to suggest that sonic art was the invention of John Cage, Edgard Varèse, Steve Reich or any other single artist. What these pioneers did, however, was to establish, in their very different ways, the belief that sound by itself could be art: the very specific ways in which music organises sound are not always wholly necessary and, as Cage suggested, given the opportunity, sound can speak for itself.

Summary

Given the substance of its foundations, it is perhaps hard to understand why it took so long for sonic art to emerge from the shadow of its ancestors. There are a number of possible reasons for this but one major factor is almost certainly the technologies that are often involved. Although (as we shall see later) not all sonic art relies upon high technologies, such methods do tend to be widely used. For as long as these remained relatively exclusive there was little possibility that the work that they made possible would be at all commonplace and therefore that it could be widely accepted.

The sampler, and later the computer, together with the related technologies of the DJ were to change all that. By making the creation of works of sonic art a less elite activity, works began to be created in greater numbers and in a diversity of forms. A new generation of artists now looked for sources and references, theories and ideas upon which to base themselves and their work. Looking back a short time showed little more than the traditional and academic practices of electroacoustic music and fine art. Looking back a whole generation brought to light the work of Cage, Reich, Varèse, Schaeffer and others. Looking back further still, Russolo's *Art of Noises* manifesto (see pp.22–23) was rediscovered, connections were recognised and the emergence of sonic arts as a form in its own right was on the way.

14. Commenting on his score, Cage explains: 'This is a score (192 pages) for making music on magnetic tape. Each page has two systems comprising eight lines each. These eight lines are eight tracks of tape and they are pictured full-size so that the score constitutes a pattern for the cutting of tape and its splicing. All recorded sounds are placed in six categories ... Approximately 600 recordings are necessary to make a version of this piece. The composing means were chance operations derived from the I-Ching.'
Cage, J. (1962) *Werkverzeichnis.* New York: Edition Peters.

15. '...giving up control so that sounds can be sounds...' Cage, J. (1961) *Silence.* Middletown: CT: Wesleyan University Press.

16. Interestingly, in his 1937 essay *The Future of Music: Credo* Cage makes a statement that seems closely to reflect Bacon's *Sound Houses*: '...Before this happens, centers of experimental music must be established. In these centers, the new materials, oscillators, turntables, generators, means for amplifying small sounds, film phonographs etc., available for use. Composers at work using twentieth-century means for making music. Performances of results. Organisation of sound for extra-musical purposes (theatre, dance, radio, film).'
Quoted in Cox, C & Warner, D. (eds) (2004) *Audio Culture: Readings in Modern Music.* New York: Continuum.

Sound Design Appears

Introduction

Sound design has a relationship to sonic arts that is quite similar to that of conventional design to art. Put simply, art seeks to represent and express ideas for their own sake. To do this, it engages with ideas, materials, media and forms of expression and communication. In this respect, it has a good deal in common with design save that design is less concerned with ideas for their own sake but sees them more as being applied to some purpose or other, be it typography, furniture, textiles or architecture. In general, we can say that art may sometimes be abstract but design is almost always concrete.

These statements are, of course, simplifications of the real situation. Here the divisions are often less clear, subjects overlap and simple definitions simply aren't enough. As in the visual world, so too in the audible one. Sonic art is not a subject that is clearly defined and nor is its relationship to sound design a simple one. There are some areas of activity, however, that are pretty clear. For example, in recent years, the sound designer has become an increasingly important member of the production team of feature films and much of the theory and practice of sound design exists in this realm. That is not to say that sound design is limited to film and television work – far from it. Designers from other areas are increasingly aware of the usefulness of sound in their work. From airports to the marketing of microprocessors, sound that is designed for a purpose is all around us. At a simple level, muzak is used in supermarkets and shopping malls to help mask unwanted noise and create an overall ambience and in a more detailed application, sonic branding is used to identify and reinforce products.

SOUND DESIGN

The creation of sound for a purpose external to itself rather than as a free-standing piece of art. Perhaps best known in relation to film and video but also extensively used for establishing and reinforcing brand identity and for other marketing purposes. The subject covers a wide range of activities and applications from the detailed practices involved in the creation of film soundtracks to the use of sound in support of other media (such as theatre, dance etc.).

The practice of sound design

The relatively recent emergence of sound design as a study and a practice might be seen as being similar to the way in which sonic art has emerged. In some respects at least, this has been as a result of the necessary technologies becoming readily available and relatively easy to use, but this view tells only a part of the story. As mentioned earlier, there is reason to believe that ancient human cultures were aware of the usefulness of sound as part of their environment and recorded history is full of support for the continued use of deliberately designed sound through the ages.

One of the most common ways in which sound could be designed or manipulated in the years before electronics was through architecture. One cannot design a structure to amplify sound: the energy that is in the original voice or instrument is all that there is. However, good design can make the most of this by focussing and concentrating the sound, or can control and modify it by reflecting it in certain ways or using resonating objects that vibrate in sympathy. History has many examples of all of these practices, from the use of masks by actors in Ancient Greece, through the stage resonators of Roman theatres (see pp.20–21), to the remarkable acoustic properties of some Mayan structures that modulate sound in ways that we would

normally think only possible by means of modern electronics.

Clearly, all these are examples of sound design having an influence on the actual architecture and construction of a building, so perhaps we can begin to think of sound design as being rather older than we originally imagined. Issues such as acoustics remain important in the design of buildings and spaces but, with the advent of electronics, it has become possible to design and hence to control not only how we hear our environment but also exactly what it is that we hear. This is the role of the sound designer.

Nowhere is the detail of what we hear more important than in film sound. Good sound design can subtly support the structure and storyline of the film, underlay the rhythm of the editing and can provide both contrast and reinforcement at every level. In doing this, the relationship between sound designer and composer is a particularly important one: the decisions of one can dramatically affect the work of the other. Equally important is the relationship between sound and vision. The two may complement each other by saying the same thing and so reinforcing an idea[17] or they may offer a contrast, even a paradox[18] (see also pp.84–85).

17. There is an elegant example of this in the Wachowski Brothers film *The Matrix* (1999). Bullets are shown in flight – in slow motion – with concentric circular shockwaves trailing behind them. The soundtrack includes the sound of real bullets being fired through multiple layers of various materials. This creates a 'zipping' sound that perfectly complements the image of the shockwaves.

18. Think here of the scene in Alfred Hitchcock's 1935 film *The Thirty Nine Steps*, in which the landlady discovers a murder. She turns to the camera and opens her mouth to scream but we never hear her: instead, we hear a similar sound – a train whistle – and the image cuts to a train rushing towards us.

'"AMBIENT MUSIC" MUST BE ABLE TO ACCOMMODATE MANY LEVELS OF LISTENING ATTENTION WITHOUT ENFORCING ONE IN PARTICULAR; IT MUST BE AS IGNORABLE AS IT IS INTERESTING.'

BRIAN ENO, 'AUDIO CULTURE'

PSYCHOACOUSTICS

The study of how we hear, psychoacoustics forms an important theoretical input to many aspects of sonic arts and particularly to electroacoustic composition. As the term implies, it includes the study of the hearing process from the perspectives of the acoustic, physical and physiological mechanisms by which we actually detect sound to the psychological and cognitive processes which allow us to decode and comprehend what we hear. Major issues in psychoacoustics include the perception of pitch, timbre and rhythm which in turn informs our understanding of 'conventional' and other musical processes such as, for example, harmony and the mathematical set approach upon which serialism is based. Additionally (and particularly for the purposes of sonic arts and sound design), psychoacoustics also includes considerations of the way in which we experience space through the agency of sound and how we locate and identify the sources of sound in the external world.

In recent times, sound design has become an important aspect of film making, gaining a degree of recognition that it has sought since the advent of talking pictures. There is one medium, however, in which sound has always reigned supreme – radio. It is odd, therefore, that with some notable exceptions, sound design for radio has tended to be taken for granted and hardly ever considered in its own right. The obvious exception to this comes in an area where sound design and sonic art overlap – radiophonics. This subject is not particularly clearly defined save that here sound is to be considered in the context of broadcasting. However, it is no longer clear quite what we may mean by the term 'broadcasting'. Traditionally, it takes the form of 'one-to-many' communication but, with the rise of internet broadcasting and the even more recent appearance of 'podcasting', this definition is fast becoming doubtful.

As mentioned before, radiophonics can fall into either category: sound design or sonic art. Here, once again, we see a clear distinction between sound that is created to serve an external purpose and a work that is freestanding and that has its own purposes and qualities. The distinction is not always quite so clear, however. For instance, the radiophonic components of *The Hitchhiker's Guide to the Galaxy* (1978) formed a crucial part of the overall work to the extent that it would be possible to argue that they were not part of the sound design for the programme but that rather, the whole programme was a work of radiophonic art – difficult.[19]

Summary

In another area, it seems that we may need to regard certain musical forms as sound design. In his early works of 🔊ambient music, Brian Eno put forward the idea that music could assume an environmental role, becoming, as it were, part of the furniture and decor if not of the architecture itself. His work *Music for Airports* (1978) acknowledges this in its very title and he suggests that he seeks to use music in much the same way as an interior designer might use colour.[20]

These examples are obvious instances of the way in which sound is deliberately designed, as part of other media or in its own right. There are other, less obvious examples of how sound is manipulated to create a particular impression such as this one from a recent review of a Subaru car:

> *Dyed in the wool Subaru fans may well miss the characteristic woofling engine note made by the unequal length intake manifolds. The STI's bigger engine, sourced from the Legacy, replaces this with a beefier exhaust sound and lots more low end torque.*[21]

It is hardly art but it could be design; sound, it seems, forms a larger part of our world than we normally realise. It creates impressions, conjures images, communicates ideas and is often as much a part of a brand identity as a visual logo.[22] It follows from this that sound design, in its many forms, has considerable potential and that it will be a significant aspect of many design activities, both now and in the future.

19. However we consider its final means of transmission, radiophonic work has one clear quality: the sound itself is all that there is. The source of the sound is hidden from us; at least we are unable to see it although we may be able to guess its nature and some of its qualities. This is a phenomenon that has intrigued people for many years. Indeed, Pythagoras coined the term 'acousmatic' to describe a sound whose source is hidden from us, and this term remains widely used (and is equally widely debated through the study of 🔊psychoacoustics) today.

20. 'I believe that we are moving towards a position of using music and recorded sound with the variety of options that we presently use colour — we might simply use it to "tint" the environment, we might use it "diagrammatically", we might use it to modify our moods in almost subliminal ways. I predict that the concept of "muzak", once it sheds its connotations of aural garbage, might enjoy a new (and very fruitful) lease of life.' Written in 1975 for the now-defunct periodical *Street Life* and quoted in Toop, D. (1995) *Ocean of Sound*. London: Serpent's Tail.

21. Review of Subaru *Impreza* 2.5 WRX STI at <http://uk.cars.yahoo.com> accessed 27/02/06.

22. Raymond Scott realised this and created a series of generic 'audio logos'. There are several examples on the 2 CD set *Manhattan Research Inc.*

AMBIENT MUSIC

A musical form that was originally designed to be part of the sonic environment rather than to be listened to in its own right. The invention of this form is generally attributed to Brian Eno who in turn describes it as (initially) the outcome of a chance event in which he was forced by circumstances to 'listen' to a recording being played at such a low volume as to be virtually inaudible except as part of the overall sonic environment. His first ambient work, *Discreet Music*, created in 1975 led to others such as *Music for Airports* (1978), which was specifically designed to be part of an environmental background.

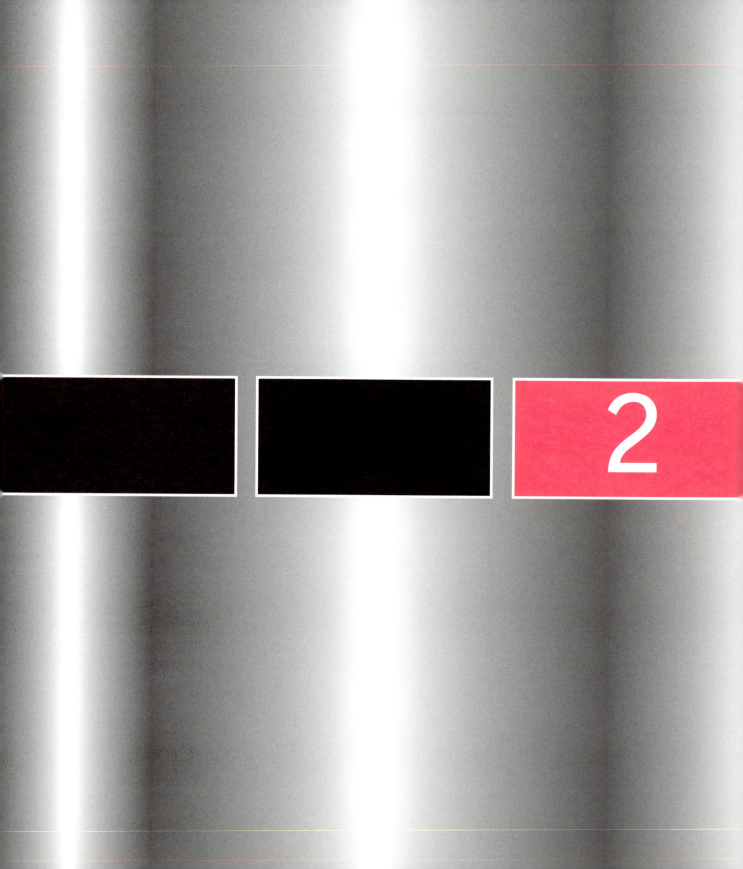

2

Artists and their Work

In this section we meet five artists whose work falls under the umbrella of sonic art. They have been chosen to demonstrate the remarkably wide scope that sonic art encompasses. We can argue the definition of sonic art from any number of standpoints: some musicians claim it to be a sub-set of music whereas, equally, some fine artists claim it as a category within their subject. Interestingly, all our interview subjects regard themselves as sound artists, despite the widely varying forms of practice in which they are involved and this leads us to conclude that such sure identity may possibly be perceived as a threat by the 'traditional' disciplines.

'THE SENSE OF HEARING CANNOT BE CLOSED OFF AT WILL. THERE ARE NO EARLIDS. WE ARE CONTINUALLY ABSORBING AND FILTERING THE SOUNDSCAPE. WHEN WE GO TO SLEEP, OUR PERCEPTION OF SOUND IS THE LAST DOOR TO CLOSE AND IT IS THE FIRST TO OPEN WHEN WE WAKE UP. THE EAR'S ONLY PROTECTION IS AN ELABORATE PSYCHOLOGICAL MECHANISM FOR FILTERING OUT UNDESIRABLE SOUND IN ORDER TO CONCENTRATE ON THE DESIRABLE. THE EYE POINTS OUTWARD AND THE EAR DRAWS INWARD. IT SOAKS UP INFORMATION.'

JANEK SCHAEFER, 'AUDIO & IMAGE'

Art or Music?

Introduction

Why should traditional disciplines perceive sonic art as a threat? To answer this, we need to consider how different forms define themselves. Traditionally, art meant painting and, possibly, sculpture. With the turn of the twentieth century and the emergence of new forms such as the 'found objects' of Kurt Schwitters or Duchamp's 'readymades', art responded by changing the definition of what forms could be considered for membership. Successively, the Dadaists, the Futurists and groups such as Fluxus pushed the membership qualifications further and further away from the original simple definitions of art, culminating in the conceptual art of the end of the century. In this respect, at least, we can argue the case for sonic art as a new form; willing and able to continue in the established experimental approach exemplified by the original avant-garde.

Music, the other main claimant to 'ownership' of sonic art, proved to be less flexible, continuing to maintain a relatively simple and limited definition of itself. Arguably, the arrival of 'Elektronishe Musik' and 'Musique Concrète' stretched the definition somewhat but, even here, established concepts and terminologies continued to hold sway and even the most 'musical' aspects of sonic art received little acknowledgement as meaningful activities.

Both music and fine art lay claim to sonic art. Clearly, it is regarded as a prize to be fought over and, given its diversity and 'tradition' of innovation, this is hardly surprising: innovation is increasingly valued in the arts, especially since older forms seem largely to have exhausted their ability to develop new responses. Sonic art re-establishes many avant-garde qualities and, in the diverse forms that their work takes, all the artists that we are about to meet undertake the search that is ultimately the focus of all art forms: to find and present '...the necessary metaphors by which a radically changing culture could be explained to its inhabitants.'[1]

1. Hughes, R. (1991) *The Shock of the New*. London: Thames & Hudson.

Vicki Bennett

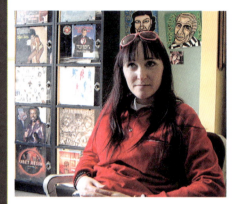

Biography

Vicki Bennett has been making CDs, radio and A/V multimedia under the name People Like Us for 16 years. She animates and recontextualises found footage collages with a witty and dark view of popular culture and a surrealistic edge, in both pre-recorded and live settings. Vicki has shown work at, amongst others: Tate Modern, the National Film Theatre, Purcell Room, the ICA, Sydney Opera House, Pompidou Centre, Sonar in Barcelona and the Walker Art Center in Minneapolis. She has also performed radio sessions for BBC's John Peel, Mixing It, and also CBC, KPFA and does a regular radio show on WFMU, called 'DO or DIY', which, since it began in 2003, has had over a quarter of a million Realplayer hits. In July 2005 People Like Us performed a concert at the National Film Theatre in London and Vicki has just finished creating a new live set. People Like Us released a DVD in late autumn entitled *Story Without End*. Funded by the Sonic Arts Network and comprising four short films, it addresses the forever-changing technology of the twentieth century. Vicki is Artist in Residence at the BBC Creative Archive. She is also making an album in collaboration with Ergo Phizmiz.

Interview

How would you describe your work?

It would of course depend on who I am describing it to, since I'd be explaining it in a way that was comprehensible and relevant to that person. My work has always involved using found sound and visual material, developed from photographic paper collage through to Photoshop and then moving image (After Effects) collage, from cut-up tape sounds and loops through to recontextualised spoken word and sample collage. This has manifested as albums, album covers, downloadable MP3s, short films, live concerts and radio productions.

Do you feel that it fits into any established category? In this respect, would you describe it as (sound) art or, given the use of other media, does it demand a category of its own?

I have called my work sound art, sonic art, collage art, plunderphonia, digital art, avant-garde music, contemporary music, short films, avant pop... actually the list is quite extensive. It is always collage, and always contextual. Or rather I always recontextualise by means of collage.

Do you use a consistent way of working or do you regard each successive work as demanding something different every time?

I make all my work on an Apple PowerBook. The sound is currently composed using Digidesign® ProTools®, and the video is made on Adobe After Effects with final editing in Final Cut Pro (see pp.92–93). This is also used in conjunction with Adobe Photoshop and Image Ready. My work is partly defined by the systems that I use. For instance I use plugins. The availability of these plugins makes a difference to what it looks and sounds like.

I ought to decide what I want to do, then find a way to do it but more often than not, I find what I have and then work with that. My editing techniques follow a certain course but each new project is approached as if I'd never done it before. The nature of found sound and visual collage is you can't tell it what to do because it already happened. You are part director and part follower. It is sometimes a very rewarding and magical process, watching for instance the way that two sources dance together, and sometimes it is annoying not being able to get them to talk to one another.

I tend to choose two sources to start with that I can somehow get to communicate with, or jar with one another. That is the starting point, and then I start to 'hang things on it'. Sometimes the source material may be very specific, like the album *Stifled Love*, where lots of people were cut off vocally from being able to express themselves in love songs, or sometimes it is very nonsensical and thrives on chaos or disobedience which leads to it being humorous.

Do you aim your work at a particular 'market' or target audience? If so, to what extent do you tailor the work to their 'expectations'?

I tend to aim it at people like myself (hence People Like Us). The aim is to elevate the mind through the various methods used in making humorous work, or by other means – using more conventional methods like emotional content. I only tailor to my own expectations, which, I guess, would be like other people's. The aim is to pick up from one point, and land somewhere else. Or at least go on a journey somewhere, and be invited to a different world.

I'm interested in the work of female artists in what is predominantly a male genre. Does this concern you and, if so, do you have any thoughts on how some sort of rebalancing might be achieved?

I don't think it's necessary to rebalance males and females in any profession. I only believe that people need to be rebalanced when people are suffering as a result. Females have as much access to this genre as males, at least in the world that I live in. I've never had a problem, so I would put a lot of the imbalance down to males naturally being drawn to making this kind of art, just as females naturally do other kinds. I don't believe in any kind of discrimination. Another reason why I'm called People Like Us is to take away such things as gender from the equation, and also to be approached and evaluated by the content of the work, not who or what I am.

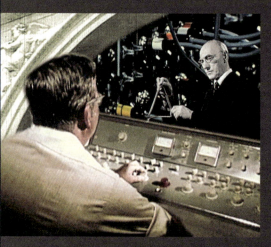

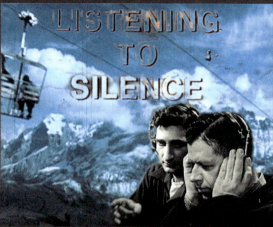

Left: 'We Edit Life'
'Experimenters in visual perception are using computers to create weird and random patterns that never occur in real life to find out what and how people see when these patterns are shown to them.'
Image courtesy of People Like Us.

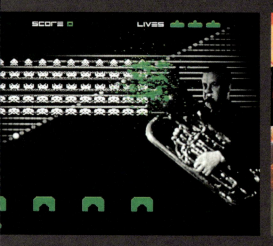

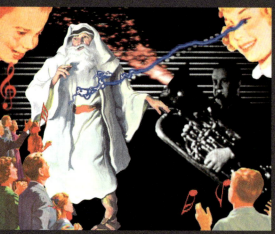

Left: People Like Us performing live
Using samples of audio and visual footage, Vicki Bennett's work is renowned for its witty and ironic take on life.
Image courtesy of People Like Us.

Right: 'The Remote Controller'
As a collage, this work can be interpreted and entered at many levels and uses narrative from a public domain film from 1950, a story that still remains relevant 57 years later: 'In amongst change there are always the very basic fundamental things that make up what it is to be human, the hope to be less isolated and to feel and do more. However, the more we surround ourselves with objects that plug us in, the more we can become disconnected.'
Image courtesy of People Like Us.

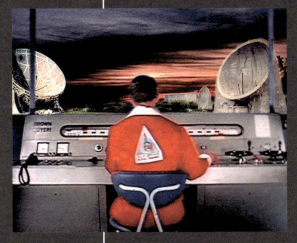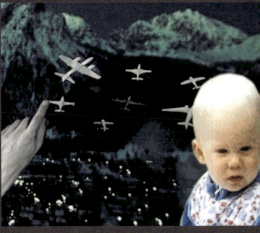

Right: 'Story Without End'
This sound and video piece samples sonic and visual footage to historically explore 'the subject of experimentation in the human body and machine interfaces — its successes and pitfalls — in the twentieth century.'
Image courtesy of People Like Us.

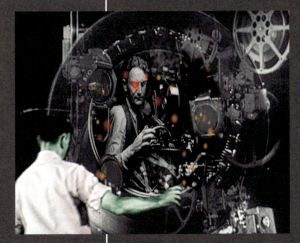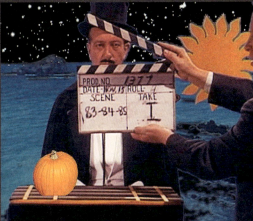

Max Eastley

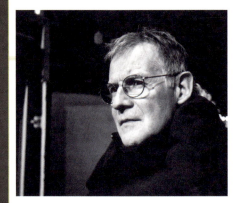

Biography

Max Eastley is an internationally recognised artist whose work combines kinetic sound sculptures and music into a unique art form. In 2000 he exhibited six installations at Sonic Boom in London and travelled to Japan to exhibit and perform with David Toop at ICC Tokyo. He was also a research fellow at Liverpool John Moores University. The previous year a permanent sculpture was installed at the Devil's Glen, Co. Wicklow, Ireland. In 2002 he exhibited at the Festival de Arte Sonoro, Mexico City, and was commissioned by the Siobahn Davies Dance Company to write music for the dance piece *Plants and Ghosts*, which toured the UK. His latest collaboration with David Toop, *Doll Creature*, was released in 2004. Also in that year he exhibited an installation at Cologne, Germany. In 2005 he created two installations in Ireland and an interior work in Riga, Latvia. In 2006 he performed with the instrument maker and musician Victor Gama, for Radio 3's *Mixing It* and will be performing with him, Thomas Köner and Asmus Tietchens at the London Atlantic Waves Festival. He is also involved in the Cape Farewell project, which brings together science and the arts to bring awareness of the effect of global warming on the Arctic environment <www.capefarewell.com>.

Interview

Could you give a description of your work?

I've always been interested in visual things and in sound, painting, drawing and music. It started out as quite a narrow sense but the third thing I've been absorbed with is movement, which is a kind of ghost, which unites them. The work I do uses movement and time as music does but it's also visual and sculptural: it uses colour and shape. So you could call me a sound artist but then that would be leaving out the visual because I do use sound in an art context: there are different contexts in which you use the same techniques and whatever context that is tends to form the subject of the work.

How would you describe your working methods?

I use the techniques of an architect sometimes – of making a mental interior model that I keep referring to, which is quite interesting. Quite a lot of composers work in that way – they see it as a kind of four-dimensional structure. I find myself thinking as a composer and a graphic artist – using drawing to formulate ideas very quickly. But really all these things need to be practised so if I'm working with music I find that I have to do a lot of music practice. When I'm working with installations, that's quite a different way of working but each one informs the other: I couldn't do my kinetic installations if I didn't play music.

If it's an installation, you have to absorb architectural things: you make a model or a drawing so you know that the space is five metres by seven and the ceiling is this height and you assemble your tools for a particular kind of work; it's like a computer – you have a particular desktop for each activity.

Is there a structure or an approach to your work that's common across all these media?

I think I'm quite unusual in that I've managed to keep all these things working without concentrating on one particular area. I see what I do as an expanding horizon: with each work, I get more height and more horizon appears which is frightening because the subject is enormous: it covers musical instruments, composition, musical forms, architecture. I don't see any edge to that horizon.

I did a work in Oxford that used a block of ice that was manufactured – it was done in layers so there was a layer of water that froze into ice and then a layer of gravel, then another layer of ice, then another layer of gravel. This was

suspended above metal plates and as the ice melted, the stones fell – you could see them hanging on so there was a tension. It was about climate change and melting glaciers.

What leads you to use technology in your work and do you sometimes find it intrusive?

I don't use it all the time but if it's necessary I do use it and you find that after you've used it, it's added another dimension. In the piece with the ice, the metal plate was amplified – it had its own speakers attached so that was a necessary part of an open-air sculpture. I find that using amplification is great if it has a degree where it goes to zero – acoustic sound – and then up to amplification so the space is gradually filled. You don't need to see what a computer is doing: it's like with architecture. To see a really good piece of architecture you don't need to see all the engineering that went into the roof before you can understand what it's doing.

In the Cape Farewell *TV programme, you were working with quite organic materials but your music track sounded very electronic.*

Some of the sounds were produced by a monochord – an electroacoustic instrument – but some of the sounds, the

bearded seal for instance, recorded underwater could be mis-interpreted as electronic sound. The Aolian harp sounds to us like feedback, but to a listener in the eighteenth century it could seem like the voices of angels. Music is defined in a technological way by recording. This is something that I found when I first started to use recordings of the work I do. If it's on a CD, it will be heard as music whereas if you hear them out in the environment, there's something else going on – it's organic, not fixed or edited. This was a huge dilemma for me when I first started recording things because I thought, 'this is not the actual work' but in a sense, it's like a photograph of the work. The definition of music in that way is 'if it's recorded and it has a duration, it could be called music'. Another definition is that it comes from inside human beings or that it comes from something observed outside. I use that as a working tool because I can relate to the emotion of music but I'm also drawn to the external, the non-human, the inanimate.

Maybe music is the personal touch and maybe the other things I do are very impersonal: with the kinetic things, you can't look at them and say that you know [anything about] the personality that made them but, with the music, you can sense me as an emotional, feeling person. So one is animate and the other is

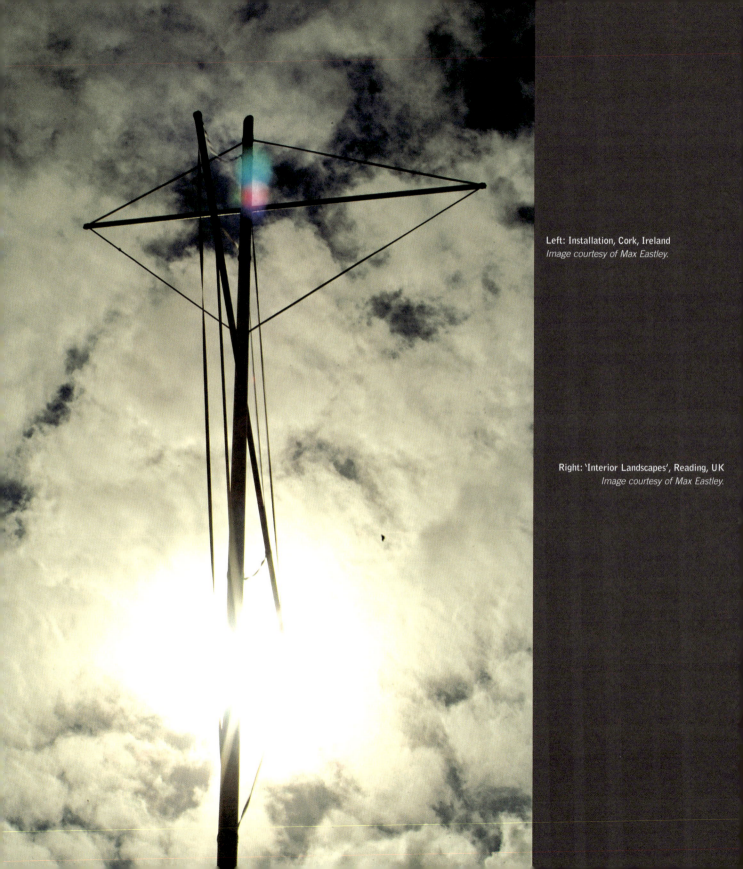

Left: Installation, Cork, Ireland
Image courtesy of Max Eastley.

Right: 'Interior Landscapes', Reading, UK
Image courtesy of Max Eastley.

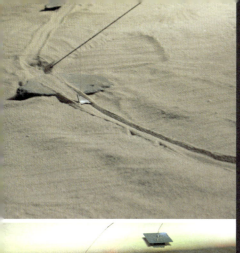

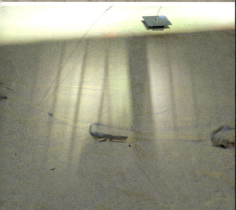

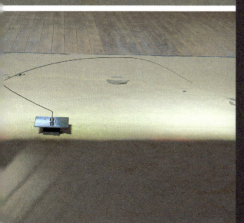

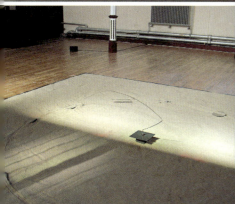

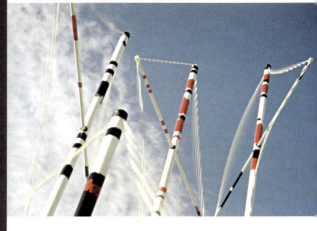

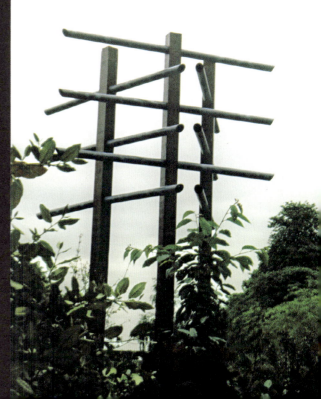

Right: Installation, Nagoya, Japan
Image courtesy of Max Eastley.

Right: Sculpture, Capel Manor, UK
Image courtesy of Max Eastley.

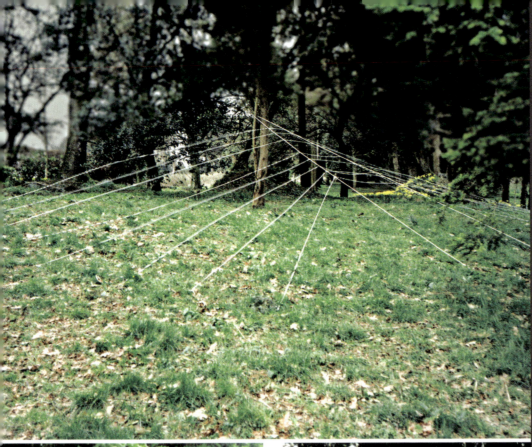

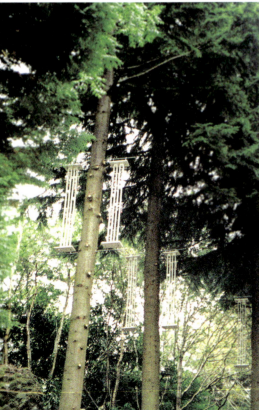

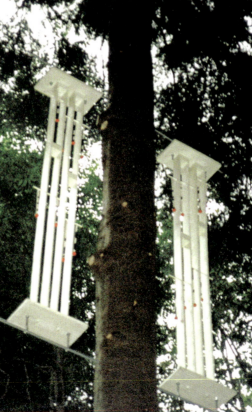

Left: Sculpture, Dartington, UK
Image courtesy of Max Eastley.

Left: Sculpture, The Devil's Glen,
Ireland
Images courtesy of Max Eastley.

inanimate – it's working with those two tensions I suppose.

Do you have a working definition of sonic art?

That's terribly difficult isn't it, because some people have defined it as something that uses loudspeakers – I can only say that I must be a sound artist because I use sound but I use it in a particular kind of way: I don't just use amplified sound. Someone once said to me 'wouldn't it be great if we didn't have loudspeakers and there was just sound and then it would be pure sound art', but I think it depends where your roots are and my foundation for making installations and things comes from kinetic art which produced sound as it moved.

Are you in the same business as, say, an electroacoustic composer?

I use electroacoustic methods and produce work that is improvised and edited afterwards. I've also been called a sound artist but that confuses people – it's that difficult word 'artist'. Aldous Huxley said 'An art form is something that an individual makes which is terribly difficult to explain to other people'. You can teach other people to do it but you can't actually define it because it's such an individual thing. There's a huge number of people that have influenced me, such as Marcel Duchamp and his definition of the 'readymade' and his methods of working using chance.

I think there's a huge amount of things that people can start listening to but there's a problem. For instance, if you want to investigate birdsong or if you want to investigate radiators, radiators are very easy to go and put a microphone against but you can't say 'I'll now go out and record the birds', because someone like Chris Watson has spent vast amounts of his life refining how you record wildlife. David Rothenberg has gone further into the area of improvising with birds – of interacting with the environment. That's one way that I see that things could expand.

The more I draw and paint now, the more I'm using sound and the textures of materials – it's a strange feedback kind of thing with me. I was always doing this but quite unconsciously but, after seeing a film of Picasso drawing, there's an extraordinary amount of measuring that he's doing by listening – it's unconscious but it makes the relationship complex.

I was painting and drawing and I took up playing the guitar and I couldn't reconcile that with the sort of work I was doing so I stopped it: there was no way those two things could exist together. Now there's a softening: there's world music and music influenced by environmental things like improvising with birds. You have the technical means to record almost anything now, when you put that into a programme, that's usable as a sculptural material – like plaster or plastic. These materials are being used to expand the idea of what music is. It's very much a late twentieth-century idea.

The world has a life of its own so why don't we listen to this world?

Janek Schaefer

Biography

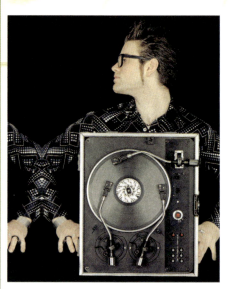

Janek was born in England to Polish and Canadian parents in 1970. While studying architecture at the Royal College of Art, he recorded the fragmented noises of a sound-activated dictaphone travelling overnight through the Post Office. That work, titled *Recorded Delivery* (1995) was made for the 'Self Storage' exhibition, curated by one-time postman Brian Eno with Artangel. Since then the multiple aspects of sound became his focus, resulting in many releases, installations, soundtracks for exhibitions (for the Urban Salon), and concerts using his self-built/invented record players with found sound collage. He has performed, lectured and exhibited widely throughout Europe, Scandinavia, North America, Japan and Australia, and won a Distinction at Ars Electronica (2004) for his random play LP *Skate*. The 'Triphonic Turntable' (1997) is listed in the *Guinness Book of Records* as the 'World's Most Versatile Record Player'. He plays in duos with Philip Jeck (Songs for Europe CD), Robert Hampson (Comae CD), Radovan Scasascia (Time and Again CD), and Stephan Mathieu (Hidden Name CD). Janek runs his own label (audiOh! Recordings) and web site (<www.audioh.com>) as well as releasing work with FatCat, Asphodel, Sub Rosa, Hot Air, Diskono, Sirr, Rhiz, Alluvial, DSP, Room40, Crónica and Staalplaat. He currently works as a full-time sound artist/sound designer/musician/visiting lecturer and composer from the audiOh! Room in London.

<www.audioh.com>

Interview

How would you describe your work?

I'm a sound artist. My work encompasses anything that uses sound usually combined with objects, space, visual art and has a close relationship with context.

Do you see it fitting into an existing category or being on its own?

My work isn't just about sound: it's about telling stories and about the world around us, doing installations etc. I don't just release it on CD for people to listen to on headphones – it dabbles in the visual arts so that half the time I'm a musician and half the time I'm an artist, but mostly both together. So I combine categories, and follow all those that come before me. I am comfortable being labelled as a 'Sound Artist'.

Does this imply different mindsets depending upon the project in question?

I have developed an overall approach as to how I tackle a commission or an idea. I divide my work into 'Head' and 'Heart', my head being concepts and heart being emotions. I try to balance the two depending on the project. I'm currently working on a piece for CD called *All Bombing is Terrorism*. I want the track to be the opposite of terror, which is often a

mental state. The music is purely a peaceful and calm opposition to war. There's a concept in there, where the emotional focus is flipped as a reaction to the context. So the head and the heart are constantly vying for attention in my work. The important thing is trying to engineer what I want the end user to understand, to experience. If I'm doing an installation, I'm thinking practically about my plugs and sockets and budgets, but in that space, do I want them to be scared or do I want them to think about the idea, or do I want them to feel happy and warm and to love life? How important is it that you understand the concept or how important is it that you just really enjoy it without having to think about it too much? I work from what I want them to receive as an experience. Ideally it should work on both levels depending on how deep you delve into the project.

Do you think that's something to do with having an architectural background?

Yes, I think it really is. When I started my architecture degree, I got my first ever A grade for my first project, because I was encouraged to do things off my own back, not just repeat things as in school. In architecture, we get set a brief, which is a situation that we have to resolve, and there are a million things that are involved

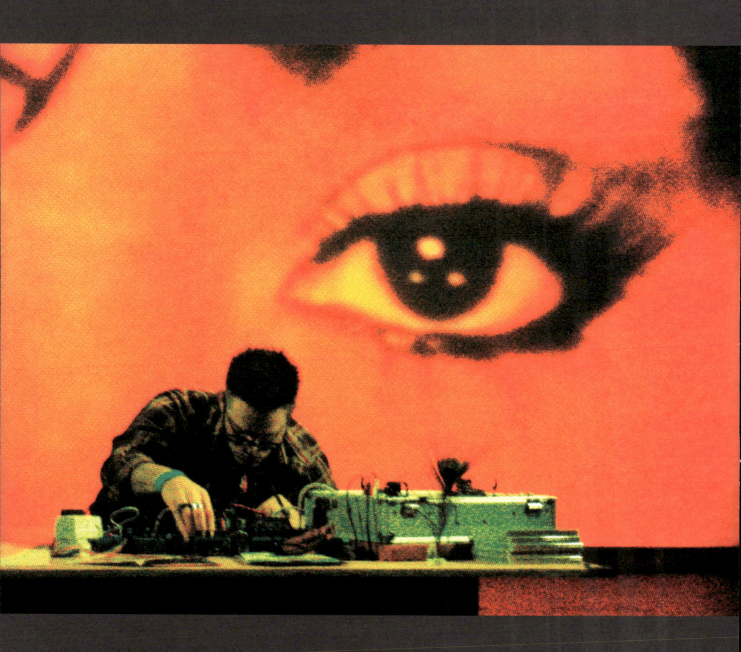

2

Left: Janek Schaefer performing live
Janek Schaefer often performs using
his self-built/invented record players
combined with objects, space and
visual art.
Image courtesy of Janek Schaefer.

in solving it, and that's how I do all my
projects – they are 'briefs' to me. I don't
for example sit down and make music for
leisure: I only do it when I've got a
deadline and I've got a reason to make it.
All Bombing is Terrorism has taken me
two years of collecting one type of loop
pedal but I hadn't plugged them all
together until someone said, 'I want you
to do this track' and I made it about the
continuous cycles of war – the historical
loop. It gave me a reason to finally use
the five loop pedals.

*How did the Triphonic Turntable come
about?*

I came up with it because I went to see a
concert by Philip Jeck, who was
performing at the RCA one afternoon
alongside Chris Watson who gave a
lecture on field recording, and Panasonic
who were creating raw, electrical,
rhythmic music. Philip showed a piece
called *Vinyl Requiem* with 180 record
players, all playing at once – a cacophony
kind of orchestra. I was trying to make
music at the time using rhythm boxes and
things because I was into techno and
electronica and DJ-ing in the Art Bar I
helped build at the RCA. I made a little
cassette album with this all-in-one Roland
MC-303 Groove Box, and at the end of it
I'd used all the sounds I liked – so I was

looking for more flexible and cheaper
options to generate sound. I then realised
that vinyl is the most physical way that
you can manipulate sound: it's tactile, it's
hands-on, you can access it all at once,
easily. You can slow it down, break it, melt
it: it's really tangible – it's just bumps in
a surface you can play with a finger nail.

So I thought there are LPs and 7"s of
every type of sound possible just lying
dormant for 10p in shops all around the
world and I thought, 'I'll do the opposite
of Philip'. I didn't fancy having to drive a
van with 180 turntables around the world
like Philip, to try and start my career: I'll
build one record player which has got lots
of record players in one unit and you can
change the sound as much as you can all
the way from 1.5 to 77.5rpm. It goes
backwards or forwards and you can play
up to three discs at the same time. It's a
very visual idea as well – people look at it
and they go 'A three-armed record player
– what does that sound like?' So you put
it on a postcard and send it out to other
people who promote gigs, then some of
them write back and you start travelling
and meeting other like-minded people and
I started my career. From the first gig I
did, I got a record deal, then started being
invited around the world and I make a
living from it now full time (as well as
being a full time ManMum).

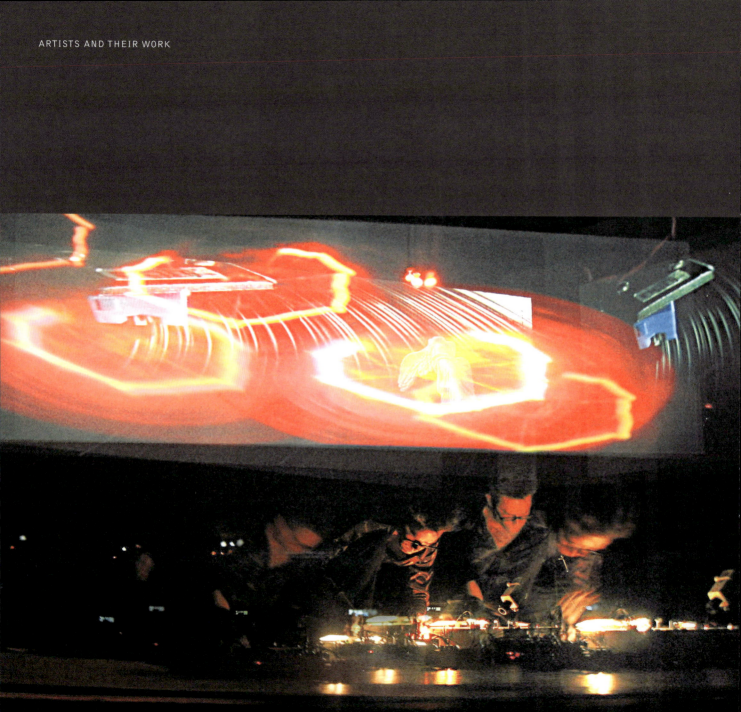

Left: Performing 'Skate'
In 2004, Janek Schaefer performed *Skate* to an audience in Linz, Germany. The original concept was to 'make a record that usurped the deterministic spiral (and the "anti-skate" mechanism) as a way of playing and listening to sound and vinyl.' This was done by cutting 'sound-scars' on to a disc with a gramophone lathe, which forced the stylus to navigate its own random path across the terrain of the physical/sonic diversions. The LP won an 'Award of Distinction' at Prix ARS Electronica. *Image courtesy of Janek Schaefer.*

Right: Performing with the Triphonic Turntable
Janek Schaefer frequently performs with his self-designed instrument featuring a three tone arm multi-record, reversible play and vari-speed turntable. *Image courtesy of Janek Schaefer.*

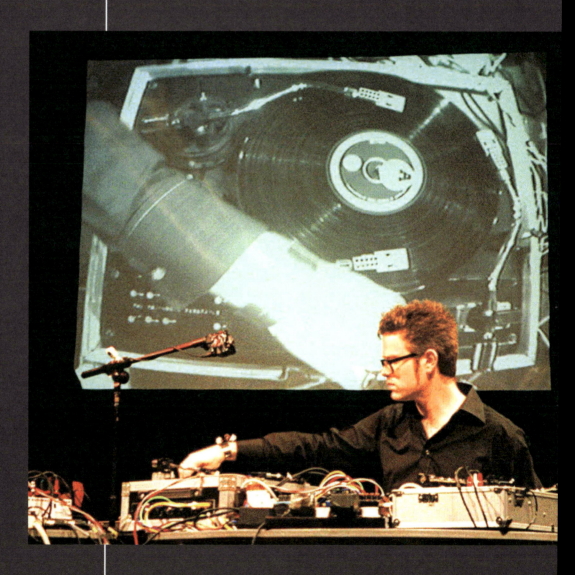

Have you created a monster?

No I don't think so, it's more of a beast! It's been in my attic now for a few years: I use my two-arm 'Twin' or 'Dual' record players because they are smaller, transport easier and don't get broken. It's not a monster or a cross to bear, because I've purposefully tried to do a range of work beyond that idea. I'm a sound artist: I use anything to do with sound, but it's what people know me for. It's out there as an icon of who I am so it's my emblem, not a monster. I moved on from it as quickly as possible really to focus on the music making which is why I built it. I was also doing installations and works like *Recorded Delivery* which was the first ever piece of sound art that I did, a great foundation. That's again just taking a piece of consumer technology and putting it through an idea and a process.

Can you say a little about relationships with technology in your work?

Technology is a tool – not the message. I don't just say, 'Hey, this is made in MAX/MSP – this is cool'; I go, 'Well you take a tape recorder and you do this with it', or, 'you take a record player and you do that with it'. It's about the idea and what you achieve with that idea. The technology sits there as a real prime focus for many projects, but it's not about the technology; it's about what I do with it.

Do you have a working definition of sonic art and how do you distinguish it from sound design?

I'm an artist that uses sound – it's as simple as that. I do concerts and installations in art galleries where I use sound as an environment – I'm a visual artist who focuses on sound. 'Sound Design' relates to particular projects, it's a trade thing – in the world where people do soundtrack composition, they're called sound designers and they put the little bits of sound here and there. For me sonic art is usually associated with installation, and composition I think. When I'm being a sound designer, I'm designing the sound in the whole space to illustrate the theme of the exhibition and thinking about it in a very 'designed' way with my architect friends. I'm designing the sound for the show and they're designing the fixtures and fittings. But when I do an installation it's my artwork that I'm producing, not fulfilling a brief for a client.

Do you feel that sound art is becoming a more public form?

I think sound art is still a small corner of the world but it's global. Audience numbers haven't necessarily been going up so I don't know if it's achieving more bums on seats. I'm still very much in a corner, but I do get the opportunity to play in big, nice places sometimes. My album sales haven't increased but my commissions have: I don't have to push for work so much now which could indicate it being more widely encouraged. Look at the number of sound courses that are popping up: I don't see that there is a big market for them to fill. Some of them will survive and it's a great education – you don't have to become a sound artist. I trained in architecture, so it's possible to use learning skills in other ways.

I've been making work with record players for ten years roughly, and there's still only around a dozen well-known people around the world who are known for experimental work with record players. It hasn't gone up to 120 or 12,000 – it's still small. People take it a little more seriously now, especially when they hear what quality of life I can lead with all the travelling, and invitations to make my work etc.

Do you see sound art developing in particular directions?

It's very broad, and I like that. There are so many ways to make it. I see that

museums are slowly making progress towards accepting it as a valid art form, and the technology has got to a state of maturity now which I think is fantastically enabling for all of us. The only reason that I can do what I do is because home computers, flights and the Internet all became affordable exactly when I started. Digital technology has developed fast, so now I can make and release albums and films at home. You can now also do almost anything with MAX/MSP (see pp.98–99), so that opens all the doors you can ever wish for creatively, if you are so inclined. I am more keen on the simpler technologies, which comes back to why did I make a three-armed record player instead of using laptop? I enjoy the physical manipulation of sound: you can't get at sound inside a computer with your hands, but with vinyl, when you play it, you see the sound being played, and you can innately understand it. So to conclude, I'd say that sound art is spreading everywhere at once, like the moss in my garden, and I love it – the varying shades give it character.

Simon Emmerson

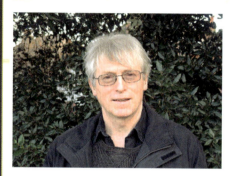

Biography

In November 2004 Simon Emmerson joined De Montfort University as Professor in Music, Technology and Innovation from City University, London. He contributes to the development of research in MTI as well as to several undergraduate modules including leading Contemporary Composition and Aesthetics. Recent music commissions include works for the Smith Quartet, Inok Paek (kayagum), Philip Sheppard (electric cello) and Philip Mead (piano) with the Royal Northern College of Music Brass Quintet, also purely electroacoustic pieces for the IMEB (Bourges) and the GRM (Paris). His works are available on the Continuum, Emanem, Mnemosyne (France) and Isidorart (Canada) labels. He contributed to and edited *The Language of Electroacoustic Music* (1986, Macmillan – still in print), *Music, Electronic Media and Culture* (2000, Ashgate) and is a contributor to journals such as *Contemporary Music Review* and *Journal of New Music Research*. He has recently completed a book, *Living Electroacoustic Music*, for Ashgate and has two solo CDs due from Sargasso in 2007. He served on the Board of Sonic Arts Network from its inception until 2004.

Interview

How would you describe your work?

I think of my work as being *live electronic* rather than *real time*: real time is a term that came in with computers and I like working with live musicians. Contrary to what's been written over the last ten years I don't believe that humans are being overtaken by technology: I believe it's possible that humans can humanise the technologies so I want to reverse the orthodoxy of the 1990s and bring humans back into the centre of our work. I think that we can remain live musicians as well as electronic musicians. Human beings are touchy-feely things whereas computers are not. I know that haptic technologies will enable us to interface rather better with computers: the first 25 years of computer music has been through some absurd interfaces not built for human interaction at all and the use of games technology is beginning to open a huge field of interactive possibilities, but I still think of the human being as a creature that is enhanced by the technology, not taken over by it.

Would you agree that electroacoustic music comes primarily from academic sources and do you feel that this an issue?

There are a large number of people who think, 'Oh that's elitist'. If they don't like the music, that's fine – it doesn't worry me, but there's a lot of high quality music being made and I think it should be valued for what it is. Many of the more radical artistic developments of the last 20 years end up in colleges and universities so it's all one big pool of possibilities as far as I'm concerned.

Do you think that the public is becoming more aware of and interested in sound art?

I'm very happy that the position of sound in our culture is so strong at the moment. When I was a student Marshall McLuhan was telling us that the visual had taken over. But I think that since that time, sound and music have moved up steadily in the public's appreciation. There's a lot more creative interaction between different kinds of music and I think that's fantastically valuable. We're in a very rich environment where people come to clubs to listen to experimental, improvised and electronic music – it's not just classic dance music. There's a feeling that quite a lot of popular music themes have run their course. We all enjoy dancing and social interaction but we also have a side that wants to listen to a kind of music that's challenging, stimulating, interesting and different. I think that's a fantastic world to live in.

Do you think that visual art has temporarily exhausted its potential and that sound is filling the gap?

We're creatures that love listening to sound without vision. Every time video technology has tried to tell us that we won't be able to listen to anything anymore unless it's got a visual attached to it, it's not been true; we love listening to sound without visual accompaniment. You can combine the two but you can listen to sonic art on its own, isolated from the visual.

Do you think that sonic art exists as a distinct form? How would you define it?

I think I probably have a different definition of sonic art than I had 15 or 20 years ago. I personally still focus it around the interaction of the human with the technology but artists such as Henri Chopin, the French concrete poet, need only a microphone and amplification. What he does is about the body and the human voice, it's not from a music tradition at all but it's certainly sonic art. Of course, sonic art can exist without electronic technology: a Tinguley sculpture, for example, is in part sonic art. I reluctantly include technological automata although I'm not so interested in automatic things but how computers and humans interact. But for me, I'm going to include electronic technology, and a kind of experimental approach to human/technology interaction.

A lot of electroacoustic work focuses upon the processes that are used to create it. What do you feel about this way of working?

I don't compose that way. Although I have an interest in a wide range of genres and styles within the sonic arts, and I have a large CD collection, I also teach composers and I don't teach all styles within the field. I have been deeply involved with the post-Pierre Schaeffer tradition of acousmatic music. I believe Denis Smalley when he says that we drive composition through the ear, that the ear perceives, that you decide intuitively how actually to put things together, even though I personally don't often compose that way – though I still try to judge the results of what I do by ear. I'm really interested in how composers put sound together and I think they don't always tell the truth about how they do things: sometimes they claim that they combine sounds just by listening (and) that they don't have any plans or formal schemes in their minds – but I find this very difficult to believe in many cases!

In 1993 I wrote a piece for harpsichord player Jane Chapman. I don't require the listener to have the slightest clue as to how I put it together but it happens to be structured through the use of Fibonacci numbers. I used these particular numbers to create a kind of organic variety of non-obvious rhythmic combination. Mozart tended to write 2, 4, 16, 18 and 32 bar structures but it was when he disobeyed those ground plans that the music got interesting. I use numerical sequences to generate musical structure because I'm interested in growth patterns and the way proportions work. I use schemas, structures and generating procedures, which I then moderate with my ears to make sure they work to my satisfaction.

If a composer uses processes, they need not be obvious to the listener. The most 'processed' contemporary music is the most popular: minimalism. Minimalism fed into some aspects of the dance revolution of the 1980s so those kinds of processes generate quite a popular surface to the music. If you take an early piece by Philip Glass or early Steve Reich (see pp.32–33), you've got processes that generate repetitive patterns or loops, which are the direct ancestors of loop programmes that young musicians are using these days to create loop-based dance music. But process can also be used to generate some fantastic music – Xenakis' music has recently been the subject of remixes by Japanese noise artists. I think this is because the statistical ideas he used link directly to ideas of noise and chaos, which act as metaphors for urban civilisation.

How do you feel about the relationships between commercial popular music and experimental music?

I'm interested in all music: I'm interested in the phenomenon known as music. I love it. I think that music is one of the most extraordinary things that humans do and I'm fascinated by how it feeds into contemporary culture as we live it now.

The world of sound to me is total: I'm very interested in environmental sound, I'm very interested in soundscape and I'm very interested in the way that humans articulate through sound. I'm interested in how sound *signifies* and that is a larger field than just music. So I think that music is a subset of sonic art and sonic art is a subset of soundscape and soundscape is really the world around us, virtually complete.

'I'M INTERESTED IN ALL MUSIC: I'M INTERESTED IN THE PHENOMENON KNOWN AS MUSIC. I LOVE IT. I THINK THAT MUSIC IS ONE OF THE MOST EXTRAORDINARY THINGS THAT HUMANS DO AND I'M FASCINATED BY HOW IT FEEDS INTO CONTEMPORARY CULTURE AS WE LIVE IT NOW.

THE WORLD OF SOUND TO ME IS TOTAL: I'M VERY INTERESTED IN ENVIRONMENTAL SOUND, I'M VERY INTERESTED IN SOUNDSCAPE AND I'M VERY INTERESTED IN THE WAY THAT HUMANS ARTICULATE THROUGH SOUND. I'M INTERESTED IN HOW SOUND SIGNIFIES AND THAT IS A LARGER FIELD THAN JUST MUSIC. SO I THINK THAT MUSIC IS A SUBSET OF SONIC ART AND SONIC ART IS A SUBSET OF SOUNDSCAPE AND SOUNDSCAPE IS REALLY THE WORLD AROUND US, VIRTUALLY COMPLETE.'

SIMON EMMERSON

Knut Aufermann

Biography

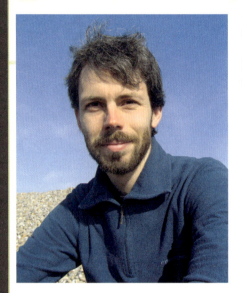

Knut Aufermann, born 1972 in Hagen (Germany), studied chemistry at the Universities of Hamburg and Potsdam. In 1998 he moved to London to study audio engineering and in 2002 gained a Master degree in Sonic Arts from Middlesex University.

From 2002–2005 he was the manager of Resonance104.4fm, London's unique radio art station, for which he has produced dozens of shows. Besides this he plays improvised electronic music in many groups such as Tonic Train, The Bosch Experience, London Improvisers Orchestra, duos with Phil Minton and Lol Coxhill as well as solo and other ad hoc combinations, with hundreds of concerts across Europe.

In 2004 he curated and played in the UK tour Feedback: Order from Noise, featuring a.o. Alvin Lucier and Otomo Yoshihide. He is currently active across Europe as a lecturer, musician, organiser, writer, curator and consultant. Recent engagements include workshops for the British Council, Dutch Art Institute and Profile Intermedia, consultancy for Radio Copernicus, lectures at the Universities of Brighton, Central Saint Martins and curation for the European radio territories project.

Together with Sarah Washington he runs the project Mobile Radio <http://mobile-radio.net>, investigating alternative means of radio production. Their works have been broadcast in 12 countries. He is also an active member of the international Radia network of independent cultural radio stations <http://radia.fm>.

<http://knut.klingt.org>

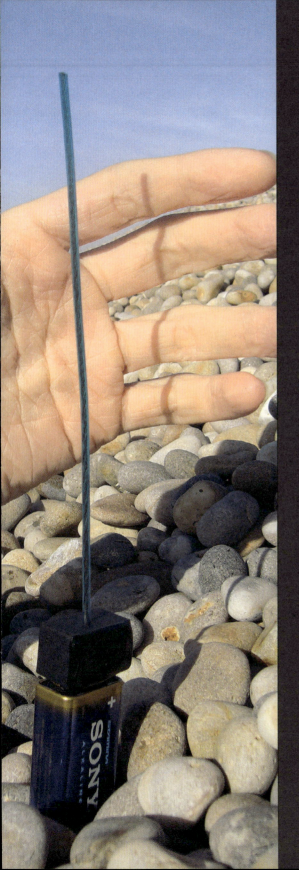

Left: Micro FM radio transmitter
Knut Aufermann is well known for his
work in radio and has now moved into
using radio in live performances too.
Image courtesy of Sarah Washington.

Interview

*There are two areas I'm interested in
talking to you about: one is radio, and
I'm also interested in the work you are
doing at the moment.*

I still do radio in terms of making radio
and I perform live, as in doing concerts,
and actually those two things start to
come together quite a lot because I
started using more and more radio
transmitters in my live performance work
so that what was, in the beginning, just
an idea of making radio and doing
experimental radio and being involved
with Resonance over the last three or four
years, has now moved into using radio on
a small scale in live performances too.

I work almost exclusively with feedback,
one of the ways is to do it with radio: you
have a transmitter and a receiver and you
send from the transmitter to the receiver
and plug the receiver back into the
transmitter. You have a feedback loop
(see pp.74–75).

*I'm presuming that there are qualities
this process gives you that the classic
microphone/loudspeaker feedback
structure wouldn't?*

Absolutely, there are a lot of things about
it. Some of it I discovered by accident, but
obviously now I can explain why these
things happen, that radio feedback has a
quality that you can't get anywhere else,

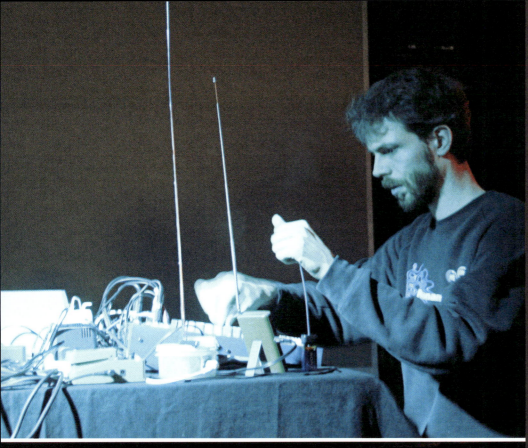

Left: Solo radio feedback performance
Knut Aufermann works almost
exclusively with feedback – often
through the use of radio.
Image courtesy of Sasker Scheerder.

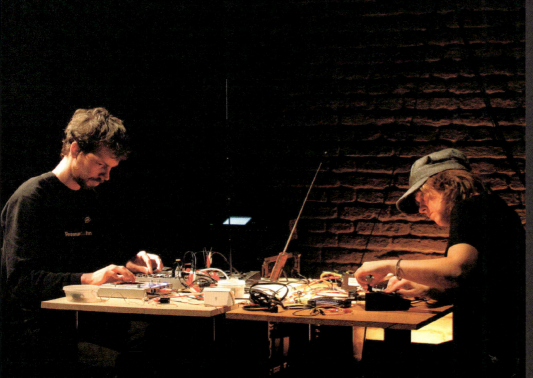

Left: Performing with Tonic Train
A live performance in Paris in 2005
using noises produced and manipulated
in real time and covering the whole
frequency spectrum – often into the
ultra- and infrasonic ranges.
Homemade electronic devices such as
modified toys, customised circuits and
ultrasonic equipment, as well as
feedback were all used.
Image courtesy of Christoph Hoefig.

it's a sound that I haven't heard anywhere else and there is also some kind of way of performing this because really you can perform quite gesturally; the capacitance of your hand changes the sound if you move it around the antennas: slightly theremin-like but much less controlled.

The word 'performance' implies particular ways of thinking about the work, particular ways of approaching it which very much have a connection with the things that inform music, so would you say that the work you did was performance in the sense that we talk about performance on an instrument?

Yes, I suppose so. In a wider sense I think this whole debate about what to call things really has something to do with who you are talking to – if you talk to people who have a very narrow defined sense of music, then you don't call it music because they won't understand it, it offends their aesthetic judgement of what music is.

Do you think that the more experimental forms that people such as yourself are involved with are about to become more widely accepted?

Certain things out of the experimental scene are going to make the step over into the mainstream. Fifteen years ago, drum and bass was seen as a completely experimental thing, and nobody would dream that thousands of people would dance to it five years later in clubs in every big city. I think there are certain things that get picked up and made fashionable and then when the fashion grows it can make the step into the mainstream. I think you can give things a little fashion index and that gives it the possibility of entering [the] mainstream maybe.

As far as I am aware, Resonance FM still remains pretty much a unique phenomenon, certainly in the UK. Can you tell us how it came about historically and how you came to be involved with it?

It's always been a project of the London Musicians Collective. It's a charity that promotes experimental music in London and further afield. The LMC is 30 years old now and in the mid '90s they started thinking about doing a radio station that actually happened in 1998 for one month. At that time, that was the only period you could get a licence for. And that really sparked something off because people enjoyed themselves massively and realised that if they had access to the medium, they would love to work with it. I was

involved at that time as an engineer and when the station got a more long-term licence in 2002 I was asked to become the station manager, which I did from 2002 to 2005. And yeah, it is something unique, it's something that doesn't exist anywhere else at the moment. It doesn't mean that there aren't other radio stations that have been around for a much longer time that are kindred spirits and that have very similar ideas, but obviously being in London it makes the whole thing very special and very different.

Does it have anything that we could call a mission statement, a vision of what it sets out to achieve?

No, I don't think so. It's got a very nice statement on the website, which starts with the words 'imagine a radio station' and it talks a lot about things a radio station could be and that maybe Resonance is in some parts. I think in a way, something that has come out of it is the radio station itself is a kind of living artwork. And that's a great thing to come out of it – it has created without actively pushing it into that way, how do you say, something that radio stations always want, a kind of identity that you can pick up very quickly without doing any corporate branding or market research, it has just developed into this.

So it almost has then, in that sense, the status of an artefact in the sense of an artist's output as an artefact, almost a physical object.

Yeah, but as a radio station, it is also so fleeting, so translocal, you can't pin it down. It puts a lot of things out but then they are gone after they have happened. I quite like that about radio, it's a whole other discussion about this whole archiving thing – this kind of holding on to things and making things into objects and storing all the data and things like this. I enjoy this thing of Resonance; it is like an old-fashioned radio station in a way. You hear a show, and you tell somebody else, if they missed it, they won't be able to hear it again, unless it gets repeated, it's not the kind of thing you have instant access to everything.

You use the term 'old fashioned' and it does sound like radio as I remember it from my childhood, yet I think a lot of people would regard Resonance as being very much cutting edge. Do you find a contradiction there?

They totally go together. I think radio as a medium has forgotten a lot of its potential that it might have had in earlier times and part of it is about rediscovering. It's the same way that I perform with small radio transmitters and make them do sounds. They've probably been around for about 80 or 90 years these things, and I'm sure somebody has used them to make sound before but it's rediscovered something. There is nothing bad about using a medium that hasn't been explored properly to do something with it that might be cutting edge.

Is there almost an element of making it all a bit magical, if you like, visiting the technology with a more innocent view, than we normally do now: is this in a sense an unsophisticated approach?

Well the technology is a bit in the background: radio is very simple to make technologically. If I sit in this studio here and I look at all this equipment and I remember being in a studio for the first time looking at this digital desk, the first thing that comes to my mind is, 'OK, how can I make it feedback?' so I start approaching the inside, because the outside, you can't touch it. I start routing things inside so that I made a feedback loop and all I got from this desk was an LED display saying this action is not allowed, so obviously I'm more interested in technology that gives me the options to do things that might be experimental without some technician who developed this desk telling me I'm not allowed to make it feed back. But the thing with radio is it is a different thing, it's all about the content, and the content is quite often not bothered by the technology.

I've always been intrigued by the breadth of content that Resonance puts to air and it strikes me that there is a nostalgic element in a lot of the material: is it intentional?

Part of it, I suppose, is because you have elderly people broadcasting so it is fair enough to have them going on about things they remember or they have memories of their youth. Another thing is there is stuff that has been produced, especially for radio, which has great content and that doesn't get aired anymore so it is a great opportunity for Resonance to collect these things and to broadcast them again, because they are great pieces of art. And this is clearly part of a view that is widely held there, that people should be actively pursuing this material and bringing it back into the public eye.

What Resonance puts out is determined by the people that make the programmes; they have complete free rein. Once they have got the programmes, they can do what they like. They decide what to do and a lot of them have this passion of things that they want to broadcast and then it becomes something that has passion and expert knowledge and, combined like this I think it makes all the quality that Resonance has.

There is clearly something of a revolution in broadcasting in general with the increased use of web streaming and podcasting. How do you think it might impact on the more experimental stations like Resonance?

For Resonance, it is great to be able to stream on the web because there is quite a bit of content that is very specialised and that you want to reach the people who are interested in it around the world. We have thousands of listeners world wide on the Web who love being able to get this specialised radio output. We do podcasts – I think it is a nice addition to the traditional method of FM broadcasting.

You said earlier that one of the attractions of radio as a creative medium was its ephemerality and yet, here we have the podcast, which is a recording. Is there something about the particular nature of the medium that gives it exemption?

The only difference I have been able to come up with so far is that with FM broadcasting, there is a possibility of accidentally tuning into something. Now that's not going to happen on the Net. You have to know where to look – you're not going to tune into Resonance by accident. The same goes for podcasts. If you know what you want, you search for the things that you want. If you're open, you just turn the dial and wait for what you get.

In your own work, is it the uncertainty of the outcome that is the appealing aspect of the process?

To play the instrument you have to use intuition rather than a kind of muscular memory, like a violin player needs. There is no intuition involved when playing sheet music: that's kind of a slight difference. I don't need to be a master of my instrument; I don't need to practise seven hours a day to become more efficient. Actually, it is more the opposite, sometimes I play concerts, three or four or five concerts in a row in a day, and by the end of it, I'm happy to put the stuff away and forget again. It can get annoying if I learn too much about how the whole thing behaves. By the time the next concert comes, in about two weeks' time, I've forgotten again and I can explore again. So I never set up my equipment at home and work with it, I just use it in the live context.

Do you see sonic art in general and radio in particular developing any specific directions in the foreseeable future?

Public broadcasters are going to do less and less experimentation and there is a new breed of radio stations or sometimes already existing radio stations on a smaller level, on a community level, that are going to embrace this experimentation maybe more than they have done before. I feel sad about these interesting things that have influenced a lot of people over the years because they heard it on public radio stations that are disappearing. But on the other hand it is a good thing: there are more and bigger possibilities for artists to go on the radio and to do something because the small radio stations open their studios and airwaves to artistic content and experimentation.

On the other hand I am also not a big fan of the people who are this big conservative thing; 'we have to keep everything as it was 80 years ago. Bring back the steam ships because they make such lovely sounds', and stuff. There is obviously development to be done in the future and part of it might be helped with radio stations that are open to the industries, but are not driven by commercial interests and are not afraid of silence and they treat their listeners as intelligent human beings who know when to switch off and know that when they switch on again there might be something interesting on.

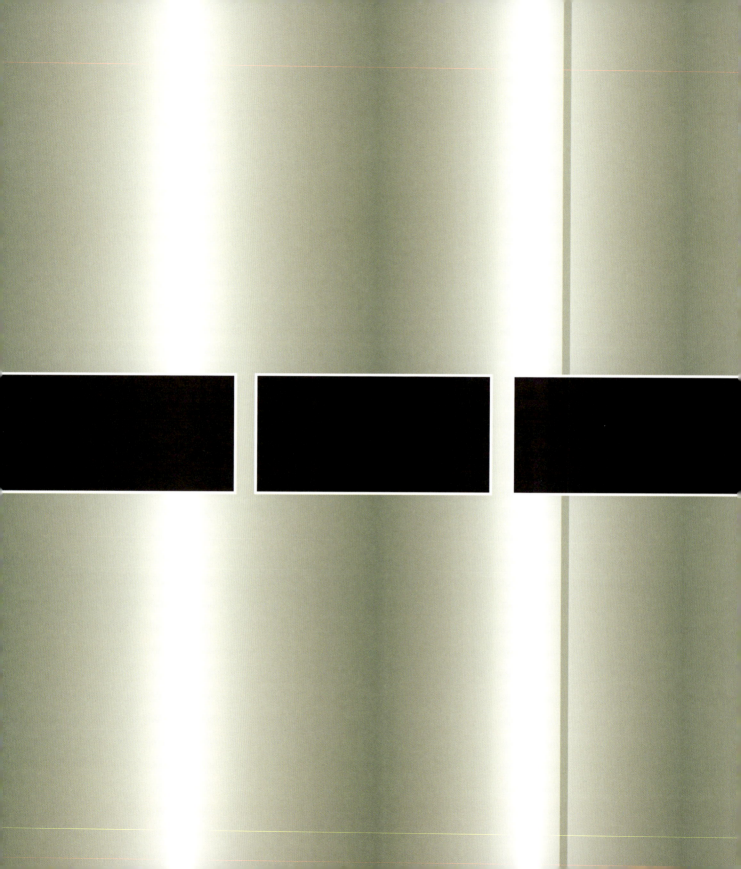

Process and Practice

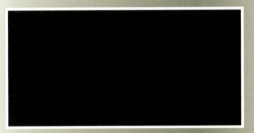

3

In this section, we look at just some of the many possible aspects of sonic art from a practical point of view. This is not to suggest that theoretical considerations are unimportant but that they are not our main consideration here. Furthermore, the range of forms that sonic art can take — from performances to recorded works to sculptures and site-specific works and beyond — is such that it would be difficult to provide a single theoretical discourse that would embrace them all. What we will do, however, is to introduce a number of practical aspects of sonic art in the hope that these will act as a catalyst for the development of individual ideas.

Studio or Laboratory?

Introduction

Recording studios exist in many forms, from the expensively equipped professional facility to a laptop computer with a couple of outboard boxes and a microphone. Conventional studio practice is not our concern here: instead we will examine a few example ideas and see how they may be deployed in a more unusual, even experimental fashion. This does not imply the need for advanced technical knowledge: what is really needed is the willingness to think outside conventional approaches and to see the subject as a series of intentions and processes rather than just technical procedures. Once we look beyond the simple cause-and-effect ideas of the recording process, we can see these resources anew: this allows us to use them in a more experimental and creative way, offering new relationships with technologies and creating a broader palette from which to work.

Iteration and feedback

By 'iteration' we mean the repeated application of a process and by 'feedback' a system in which part of the output is recycled back to the input to be processed again. Clearly the two ideas are closely related and both are extensively used in recording and performance.

The simplest form of sonic iteration is via a time delay such that the original sound is heard and then, after an interval, is heard again, i.e. a simple, single echo.[1] It is easy to arrange a feedback structure around this delay so that the echo is returned to the input to be delayed and heard again.[2]

If the level of feedback is low, each iteration will be quieter, so the sound will gradually die away. If it is above a certain level, each iteration will become louder until the system reaches the runaway state that we refer to as 'feedback'. There is no need for a delay in order to create feedback – most amplified systems can be

1. Iteration of a time delay process is just one possible form: any process can potentially be applied repeatedly. In Alvin Lucier's work *I am sitting in a room* (1969), he records himself speaking a prepared text. The recording is then played back into the room and re-recorded with a microphone. In this process, the original recording is 'coloured' by the resonant qualities of the room. This 'coloured' recording is then played back into the room and recorded again, doubling the intensity of the effect. The process is then repeated over and over until the original words have become unintelligible and all that is left is the rhythmic pattern of the speech and the resonant qualities of the room itself.

2. An example of this is the echo typically used on the vocals of many early rock 'n' roll records. This was achieved by using tape recorders, exploiting the delay between the recording of a sound by the record head and its reproduction by the play head located an inch or two away. The delay created was a function of both this distance and the speed of the tape.

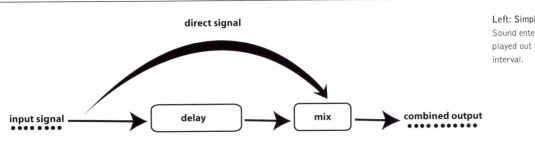

direct signal

input signal → delay → mix → combined output

Left: Simple delay system
Sound enters, is stored and then played out after a variable interval.

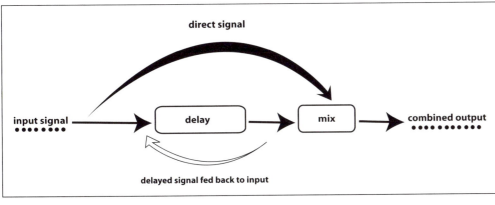

direct signal

input signal → delay → mix → combined output

delayed signal fed back to input

Left: Delay system with feedback
Sound enters, is stored and then played out after a variable interval. Part of this delayed sound is returned to the input to be delayed again.

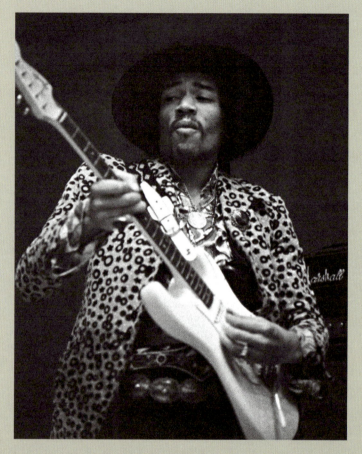

Above: Jimi Hendrix
Jimi Hendrix's playing shows some of
the most outstanding examples of the
creative and dramatic use of feedback
processes.
*Photo © Kim Gottlieb-Walker, all rights
reserved, <www.lenswoman.com>.*

persuaded to feed back[3] — however, the
conventional view is that it is something
to be avoided!

Feedback can be used to dramatic effect
as a creative process and the work of Jimi
Hendrix provides one of the most
outstanding examples.[4] It has been said
that Hendrix did not simply play his guitar
but also his amplifiers and speakers —
what we would nowadays call a
◁ᵕ⁾'hyper-instrument'. The core principle of
his sound was simple: the guitar string is
plucked and vibrates and this is turned
into an electrical signal. The amplifier
boosts this signal and the loudspeaker
replays it. Normally, the vibration slowly
dies away but, if amplified enough, the
vibration from the loudspeaker will cause
the string to vibrate in sympathy. Below a
certain level, the sound will still die away
(although more slowly — giving rise to
what guitarists term 'sustain') but beyond
that, the vibration will build up as the
feedback process takes hold. This will
dramatically alter harmonic content and
hence the overall sound, providing the

player with a whole new range of tonal possibilities.

The uses of iteration are not limited to sustain and tonal enrichment: it can also provide both rhythm and structure and this has been exploited by a number of artists. Early tape works by Steve Reich (see pp.32–33) used the repetition of pre-recorded material to create complex shifting interactions and this same complexity of structure and texture became a signature part of performances and recordings by Terry Riley. Riley uses delays and repeats as part of his compositional process, allowing him to play a new musical part against one played previously but still cycling through the delayed feedback structure of his system. This originally used tape recorders but, in later works, digital units.

Another notable exponent is British guitarist Robert Fripp, who used Riley's basic ideas to create his own system, 'Frippertronics'. Originally this used two tape recorders to provide the delay. This

3. See for example, Steve Reich's work *Pendulum Music* (1968). This work is part installation and part performance in concept and has a microphone suspended above a loudspeaker (or loudspeakers) to which it is connected via an amplifier. Feedback is created by this system but is modulated by the swinging of the microphone, until the microphone/pendulum comes to a stop and a single continuous tone remains.

4. Hendrix did not invent feedback as a technique – the first example I heard was on The Beatles' 1964 recording *I Feel Fine* in which the first note is struck with the instrument volume relatively low. This is then turned up quickly, creating a sudden dramatic snarl of feedback after which it reverts to normal as the song takes over. It is hard to imagine how dramatic an impact this unexpected sound had upon the record-buying public, many of whom regarded it as a fault that had been carelessly overlooked, rather than a genuine sonic experiment.

HYPERINSTRUMENT

A hyperinstrument is one that is made up of a number of components which, acting together, form a whole that is greater than the sum of the individual parts, but which nonetheless acts as if it is a single instrument (albeit one with exceptional qualities). Thus the guitar is normally thought of as a single instrument but Hendrix and others combined its inherent qualities with the volume and tonal modification of loudspeakers and the electronic impact of amplifiers to create a feedback-based system. This was essentially a single instrument, which, despite consisting of a number of independent parts was under the control of a single performer and was played as a whole, rather than having those parts each controlled separately.

delay was, however, far longer than that achieved by exploiting the gap between record and play heads. Frippertronics increased the delay by running a single reel of tape from one machine (which would record the sound) through to a second machine that would play it back. The distance between the machines determined the delay and this rate of repetition determined the overall structure of the piece. Once again, later forms of the system abandoned tape delay for the more reliable and flexible technology of digital electronics.

A consistent collaborator with Fripp has been producer Brian Eno, who is generally credited with 'inventing' ambient music and creating some of its early works such as *Discreet Music* (see pp.38–39). This uses a technique very similar to that adopted by Riley and Fripp.

These are examples of how iteration and feedback can be used to create fascinating and complex sonic structures. It is, of course, possible to go further and to cascade processing units together. Here we enter hazardous but exciting territory: the outcome is almost wholly unpredictable so there is a need to record everything, since the interdependence of the components is so complex as to make reproducible results impossible. This is a fascinating area to explore and indeed it is perfectly possible to create extraordinary results using only the noise inherent in the electronics of the system as the source.[5]

There is no requirement for expensive and complex equipment. Large studio processors are immensely powerful and flexible but equally interesting results can be achieved with simpler and cheaper units. Whichever approach one takes, this is an exceptionally rich source for sonic experimentation.

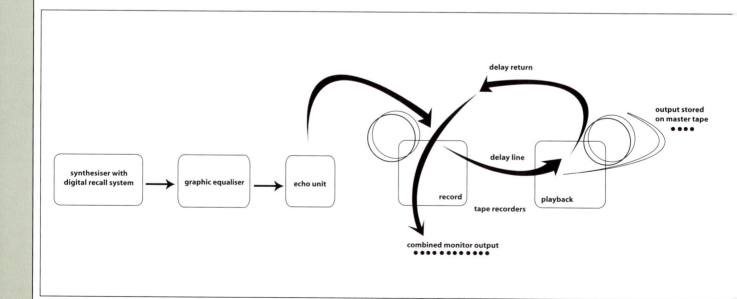

5. See the work of David Lee Myers <www.pulsewidth.com> and his 'Feedback Workstations' or that of Toshimaru Nakamura <www.japanimprov.com/tnakamura> whose work involves connecting the output of a mixer directly back to its input. These two approaches produce entirely opposite results: Myers' system creates a high degree of complexity whereas the approach taken by Nakamura tends to reduce the final sound to a very simple form indeed.

Left: Brian Eno's 'Discreet Music'
The sound generated by the synthesiser (controlled in turn by a digital sequencer) is processed through a graphic equaliser and then subject delays and iterations from the two tape recorders.

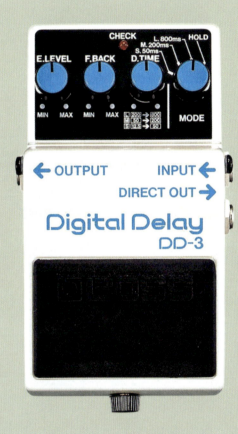

Above: Boss DD-3 guitar pedal
A simple but versatile digital sound processor capable of a useful range of time-based effects.
Image courtesy of Roland Boss UK Ltd.

Articulation

One of the most fundamental activities of sonic art involves examining individual sounds to see what they are made of and what they relate to. Thus we discover much about their nature and meaning: it is rarely sufficient to present a sound 'as is' since this tells us only what is on the surface, not what the sound is made of at a deeper level or what its relationships may be.

Before we examine the context in which we hear a sound, we need to consider how to discover its structure and there is no better way of doing this than identifying its components and seeing how best to display them. This is known as articulation and we can approach it in two main ways: firstly, we can be analytical and uncover the components that make up a sound object and, secondly, we can use another sound as a means of discovering how it interacts with others.

Both approaches help us to understand what our sound consists of and what it may signify: both can be undertaken using regular studio technologies. A number of possible processes could be adopted: for example the filter of a synthesiser allows us to isolate and hear each individual harmonic. Here we consider two other examples: the (noise) gate and the vocoder.

For our purposes, the gate is the most useful of the several types of dynamic processor. One quality is common to all: the level of sound passing through the unit is subject to automatic control. This is usually derived from the sound itself or via a 'side chain' carrying the same information. However, there is no reason why this has to be so: the controlling element can be derived from another source so that one sound is subject to the 'articulation' of another.

Right: The Behringer Multigate Pro
A simple dynamics controller capable of a useful range of processes.
Image used with permission of BEHRINGER International GmbH © Copyright 2006. BEHRINGER International GmbH.

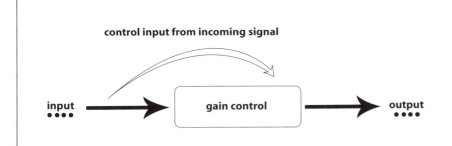

control input from incoming signal

input

gain control

output

Left: Simple dynamics processor
The incoming signal directly provides information used to control the level of the output.

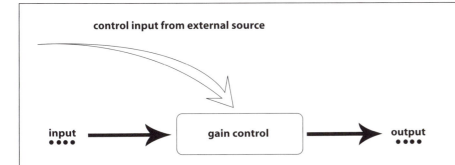

control input from external source

input

gain control

output

Left: Dynamics processor with side chain
The information used to control the level of the output normally comes from the incoming signal but can be derived from another source allowing the dynamics of one sound to be imposed upon another.

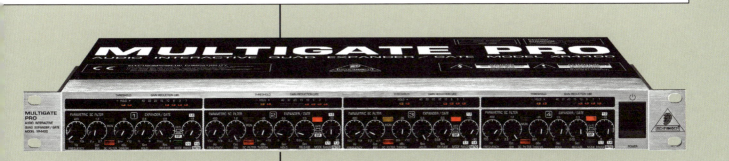

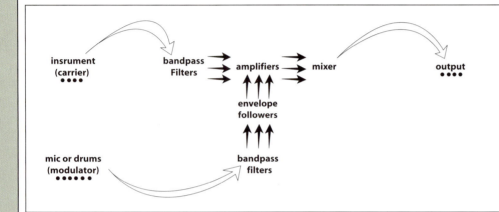

insrument
(carrier)
••••

bandpass
Filters

amplifiers

mixer

output
••••

envelope
followers

bandpass
filters

mic or drums
(modulator)
••••••

Left: Diagram of a vocoder
Vocoders allow one sound (the carrier) to be articulated by another (the modulator).Unlike dynamics processors, vocoders analyse energy levels at a number of frequencies in the modulator signal and apply the results to equivalent frequency bands in the carrier signal.

A gate usually passes no signal unless its volume exceeds a set level. In normal use, it is our chosen sound that opens and closes the gate for itself but we can use another sound for this purpose: applying our second sound to the side chain will open and close the gate independent of our original sound thereby articulating one sound by another.[6] This can tell us a great deal about the dynamic structure of both sounds.

The gate offers a useful form of articulation but works very simply upon sounds as a whole. A more sophisticated (although essentially similar) approach is offered by a vocoder. Like the gate, the vocoder allows one sound (the carrier) to be articulated by another (the modulator) but there the resemblance ends: the vocoder takes the modulator signal and analyses it for energy at different frequencies. It takes this information and applies it to filters and envelope followers that act upon the carrier as shown in the diagram.

Traditionally, the vocoder encodes the human voice upon something else, usually resulting in crudely 'singing' synthesisers.[7] A little imagination will suggest that this approach can be far more versatile: it can encode any sound upon any other – arguably the ultimate in articulation.

6. A particularly good example of this occurs on the track *Fire* on the 1977 album *Consequences* by Kevin Godley and Lol Creme. Here, the cracklings and poppings of a fire are used to trigger a noise gate that is carrying a vocal track singing the word 'fire'. Hence the word, with all the meaning that it has for us, is apparently articulated by the sound of the actual fire itself.

7. There are other means by which instruments and other sound sources may be made to speak or sing. A simple approach plays the sound back through Walkman earpieces or via a tube, both of which are placed in the mouth. The user then shapes the desired words or sounds silently and his/her vocal track takes on the function of a (rather limited) vocoder. Other approaches include using transducers to artificially excite the vocal chords. Most famously used to create *Sparky's Magic Piano,* these are also used to provide an alternative to natural speech for patients who have undergone surgery on their larynx.

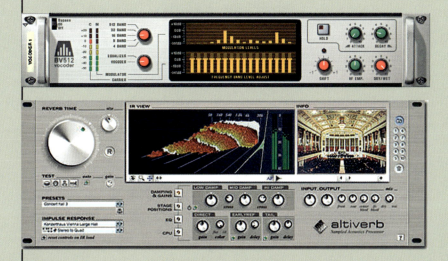

Above, top: Software vocoder
This software vocoder is made by Propellerheads.
Image courtesy of Propellerhead Software AB.

Above: Altiverb
A hardware or software reverberation system using convolution processing to impose a sampled acoustic upon the incoming sound.
Image courtesy of Audio Ease.

Space and place

Having created a sound, we need to present it. Conventional studio practice takes very little notice of this beyond adding a little treatment and reverberation (see also pp.36–37). This denies us a useful opportunity – that of hearing our sound in relation to a real or imaginary environment; placing a sound in an acoustic space can do much to reinforce or contrast with our expectations.

The basic technique here is reverberation: many systems exist that simulate real and imaginary environments and the best of these are capable of excellent performance. Where many fall short is that they create 'spaces' that are impossible or unbelievable and, whilst these are immediately attractive, their artificiality may make them unsatisfying in the longer term.

The space in which a sound is performed and heard can dramatically influence the way in which we perceive and respond to it,[8] hence the need for spaces to be believable. Rather than attempting to simulate the acoustics of a real space, convolution allows us to sample the actual qualities of a space and to use them as a matrix in which to embed our sound. Thus it is possible to place a sound in the acoustic of London's Albert Hall or the dome of the Taj Mahal. Convolution systems find wide application not least since one can make a location recording of a chosen acoustic space and can then 'place' one's own sounds in it.

Having established a location for our sound, we need to consider how to place it there. A stereo recording allows us to locate it on a line between the speakers. A surround system adds the element of front/back allowing us to locate on a flat plane but neither approach allows us to indicate the distance of our sound from the listener. In landscape painting, two ideas are used to indicate distance: an object that is far away will appear bluer in hue and paler in tone than one that is closer (as happens in nature). We can adopt a similar tactic: a sound that is far away will have more reverberation than one that is close by (increased blueness) and will have less high frequencies (a paler tone). Again, this is a reflection of nature: a distant sound assumes more of the acoustic qualities of its location and is muffled compared to the 'dryness' and 'crispness' of a close one.

Locational provenance confirms the status of a classical recording (see pp.20–21) and the ephemerality of much recorded rock and pop music has been attributed to a tendency to opt for acoustics that are spectacular rather than credible. In the case of Jimi Hendrix (see also pp.76–77), the placement of microphones in the studio and the sense of space and place that was communicated by powerful amplifiers and speakers making large amounts of air move in a big room was crucial to conveying the essential qualities of the performer and his work. In establishing recorded sound works as serious art endeavours, it costs us little to ensure that the sounds that we create are appropriately placed.

Summary

As we have seen, the technologies and working practices of the conventional recording studio can appear, superficially, to be very close to those of sonic art and sound design. This proximity is, however, somewhat of an illusion. Certainly, some of the same equipment is used but the critical difference is how we answer the question of what informs its use. The recording process as it applies to conventional music is a well-established pathway of practices that leads to a consistent series of outcomes. The use of studio technologies in the creation of sound art is quite different: Brian Eno has observed that he finds it perfectly acceptable to enter the studio with absolutely no ideas in his head and simply to let himself be driven to work in particular ways and with particular process in response to what he hears. This is perhaps an extreme difference and most sonic arts studio practice lies somewhere between the two poles. The interesting difference is the focus upon the qualities of sounds in their own right without there being any inevitable reference to their 'musical' context. We should, however, be careful in making unduly clear-cut distinctions. In his book *Audible Design*, Trevor Wishart refers to what he calls 'sound composition' as a practice that partakes of both the experimentalism of sonic art and of the conventions of musical composition and this may form a basis upon which we are able to re-visit the practices of recording as we have known them hitherto.

8. Listen, for example to *Inside* – Paul Horn's 1968 recording of improvised flute playing under the dome of the Taj Mahal. Not only does the feedback that Horn receives from the acoustics of this space impact upon his playing but the personal and cultural significance of the Taj Mahal also colours our response to what we hear.

Designing and Creating Sounds

Introduction

Here we look at some of the many ways in which we can create sound but, perhaps more importantly, how we can use sound as a means for the communication of ideas. This is an important issue for all areas of sonic arts practice, although the need to transmit detailed information is relatively more common in radiophonics or film sound design than in such areas as electroacoustic composition where process and/or overall impression are perhaps more important.

When we use sound to communicate information or to represent something descriptively we need to pay particular attention to the expectations of the audience: these are, in part, conditioned by exposure to media and hence they may have quite specific expectations. They will often have no direct experience of what something *actually* sounds like but nonetheless have highly developed expectations of what it *should* sound like. Our problem is to decide how highly we value authenticity and to what extent we are prepared to be pragmatic and give the 'public' what it wants.

Analysis and synthesis

It is possible to use a wide variety of sources and processes in the creation of a composite sound. In order to do this effectively, we first need to adopt an analytical approach: to consider what the actual components of our sound are. For example, if an old aeroplane has four engines, everything needs to be four layers deep, each at a slightly different timing and pitch. The engines make a noise in their own right but much of the noise is made by propellers stirring the air – so we need to give the sense of air in violent motion – and a general background rumble. All this implies quite a number of components to create a composite sound.

This is typical of the approach of the sound designer: a willingness to analyse what the components of the sound might be and then to find ways of acquiring them. We can make field recordings of actual environments and particular sounds, we can process and transform them through studio technologies, we can articulate sounds by means of each other and we can create new sounds from scratch by means of synthesis. Increasingly, we can combine any or all of these methods but these tools are only useful if applied intelligently and

purposefully and this in turn requires the initial analysis and also perhaps a degree of lateral thought.

As we have seen, an important part of any such process is ensuring that the sounds we create are presented in the right context. My imaginary plane could not sensibly exist in a studio, so the basic recordings need to be bedded in a soundscape of noises that suggest the background bustle of an airfield, thus placing the main sound elements in a context that enhances their credibility. The question always has to be, 'if I were really there, what exactly would I be hearing?'.

New systems have dramatically improved the art of location recording. These can often be connected directly to a computer and the recordings then appear as sound files that can be imported into editing and assembly programmes such as Audacity or Digidesign® ProTools®. This is a quick, direct and simple process for acquiring real-world sounds and the all-important background environments that will help to make designed sounds believable.

Sometimes, real-world recordings need a little modification to help them fit their

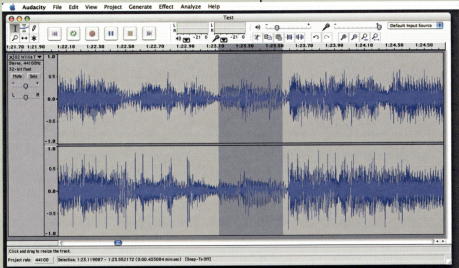

Left: Audacity
A useful shareware sound editing programme available for all main operating systems.

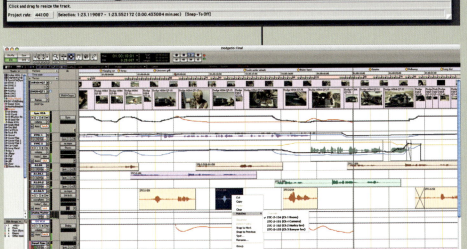

Left: Digidesign® ProTools®
The de facto industry standard for multitrack audio recording, editing and processing.
Image © 2007 Avid Technology, Inc.
All rights reserved.

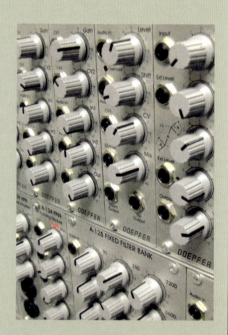

Above: Part of a large modular analogue synthesiser
Middlesex University's Doepfer A-100. Adopting the voltage control techniques originally developed by Robert Moog, such systems give users direct access and wide-ranging control over almost all parameters of a sound.

purpose: for example, a close sound can be rendered more distant by making it slightly muffled and more reverberant. In general, such modifications can be accomplished using the basic tools of the recording studio, but sometimes more specialised operations such as time stretching or pitch changing are required and here the computer becomes an invaluable ally. The latest software technologies are undeniably hugely powerful but there is also much to be said for a simpler approach and synthesis is a good example of this.

Modern synthesisers often exist as software and many of these are excellent in what they do. They are also capable of integration with recording and sequencing software such as Cubase, Logic or Dididesign® ProTools® and this provides a cost-effective one-stop resource for making and modifying sounds. There is also a strong case to be made for a more 'traditional' approach and here nothing beats an old-fashioned modular analogue synthesiser for sheer flexibility, since most such systems can be used to process existing sounds as well as to create new ones. However, there are some areas of

sound at which these older approaches perform poorly and newer digital systems are superior. This is particularly the case with percussive sounds and harmonically complex ones such as voices.

A number of excellent software synthesisers cope very well with these demands but the most versatile solution is provided by a programming environment such as MAX/MSP or Reaktor. MAX/MSP is hugely powerful but takes what is perhaps a somewhat sledgehammer approach and suffers from a rather steep learning curve. Reaktor and other software programmes such as Absynth and Reason provide user-friendly approaches and cope well with the majority of such demands. Reaktor, in particular, has become a firm favourite amongst film sound designers.

There are a number of different approaches to sound 🔊synthesis and each has its own characteristic (and often identifiable) qualities that can make it more-or-less suitable for particular purposes: there is no overall 'best' system so knowledge of the qualities of each is highly desirable.

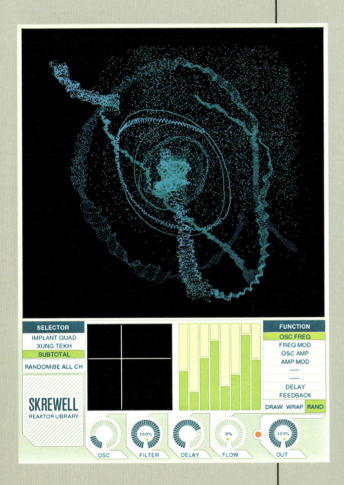

Left: Reaktor
A software synthesis and sound
creation programme much favoured by
sound designers.

SYNTHESIS

There are a number of approaches to the
electronic synthesis of sounds. The main division is
between analogue and digital systems. Analogue
systems use traditional electronic systems such as
oscillators, filters etc. to directly generate pitched
and unpitched sounds and to process them in a
range of ways – modulating frequency, harmonic
content and amplitude. The most common
approach is known as 'subtractive synthesis' where
parts of a harmonically rich waveform are
removed, leaving only the desired components. This
approach stems from the early work of composers
such as Karlheinz Stockhausen (who used
laboratory test equipment) and the later creation
of the synthesiser, most notably by Robert Moog.

'A VIDEO CAMERA IS CLOSER TO A MICROPHONE IN OPERATION THAN IT IS TO A FILM CAMERA: VIDEO IMAGES ARE RECORDED ON A MAGNETIC TAPE IN A TAPE RECORDER. THUS WE FIND THAT VIDEO IS CLOSER IN RELATIONSHIP TO SOUND, OR MUSIC, THAN IT IS TO THE VISUAL MEDIA OF FILM AND PHOTOGRAPHY.'

BILL VIOLA, 'DIGITAL & VIDEO ART'

Designing sound for film and video

As mentioned earlier (see pp.36–37), the importance of sound design in films and television has steadily increased in recent years. There are a number of reasons for this, especially the complexity and performance of cinema sound systems and, increasingly, the availability of relatively sophisticated surround sound systems for domestic use. Both these factors lead to a demand from consumers for higher quality sound and hence an increased sense of spectacle. It is the role of the sound designer to take responsibility for a huge and often under-rated proportion of the narrative, mood and emotional content of a movie and to reinforce or contrast with its visual design to create a single effective whole. In his excellent book *Sound Design*[9], David Sonnenschein writes:

The true sound designer must be immersed in the story, characters, emotions, environments and genre of the film. With their contribution the audience will be led down the path in an integrated, yet most often subconscious manner toward an experience that is authentic and human, a metaphor for the life experience itself. Using all the tools of music, psychology, acoustics and drama, the art of orchestration comes into play, selecting the right sound for the right moment. The sound designer performs a balancing act between making the best aesthetic choices and the technical parameters of completing the film on time, in budget and with the tools and personnel at hand.

This suggests that the role of the sound designer has moved from the periphery to the heart of the filmmaking process. Where once it was merely something added in the late stages of post-production, sound design is now a process that begins before an inch of film has been shot and continues until the completion of the final mixes. Effective sound design provides detailed reinforcement of and contrast to visual elements and perspectives. It also adds elements that do not exist at all in the visual component and contributes to the cycle of tension and release.[10] It has become an integral and crucial part of the film design process as a whole as well as moving to a central position in the narrative of the film.

Sometimes the process is simple and ingenious but is very often of huge complexity: for example, the final mix of Arnold Schwarzenegger's *Terminator 2* used banks of synchronised digital multitrack recorders, making a sum total

9. Sonnenschein D. (2001) *Sound Design*. Studio City, CA: Michael Wiese Productions.

10. A colleague recently showed me an extract from Roman Polanski's 2002 film *The Pianist* in which a tank is shelling an apartment building. We hear and see the tank approaching but, unusually, we hear the whine of the motors that elevate and traverse the gun. The tank fires a shell and we cut to the interior of the building. We can no longer see the tank but suddenly we hear the whine of the motors again and know that the tank has retrained its gun upon our location. This builds an extraordinary level of tension over the next few seconds until the inevitable explosion comes. The sequence ends with the addition of a high-pitched whining noise – exactly the sound of the ringing in the ears that most of us experience after exposure to a sudden loud noise. The subjective realism is quite remarkable and almost entirely a function of the award-winning sound design work of Jean-Marie Blondel, Gerard Hardy and Dean Humphreys.

Summary

of over 100 tracks of audio material linked together and fed through a huge mixing console. These would now be replaced by computer systems storing material on large hard drives but the mixing and dubbing process would be no less complex. By no means the least consideration for the sound designer is how the film will sound in the multiple forms in which it will finally appear; from the complicated multichannel presentations of the major cinema to the simpler systems of the provincial outlet, to the domestic 'home cinema' and finally to the 🔊stereo (or mono) televised version.

Increasingly, film and video technologies are converging and this can be an asset to those working with sound. Both audio and video editing software are based upon a visual timeline and this means that it is

relatively straightforward to coordinate sound to vision at a practical level. Software designers have done much in recent years to facilitate this process and integrated suites of software are widely available, offering a considerable advantage over the synchronisation of separate video and audio systems that was previously the only way in which such work could be carried out.

In these examples, we can see that basic editing work can be undertaken on the soundtrack using the video editing programme but, where detailed processes are required, it is a simple matter to switch into the sound programme, make detailed adjustments and drop back to the 'main' programme all with a few clicks of the mouse.

Interestingly, these programmes are also readily integrated with animation and image processing applications, all of which put sound into a far more level relationship with visuals and confirms the centrality of the role and crucial responsibilities of the sound designer. The film industry increasingly acknowledges this change in situation and this is also reflected in the developments of technologies that have taken place over the last few years. Sound and image are, to an ever-increasing extent, handled in broadly similar ways and we may speculate that the days of a fully converged multiple medium may not be far away.

Right: Apple Motion
An animation application designed to be used in conjunction with Final Cut and Soundtrack.
Image courtesy of Apple.

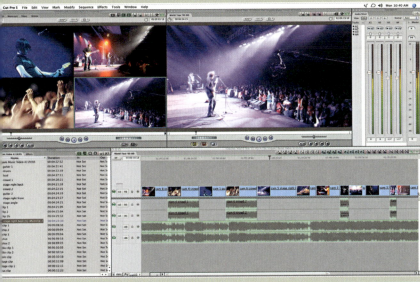

Left: Apple Final Cut Pro
A widely used video editing application
with multiple audio tracks.
Image courtesy of Apple.

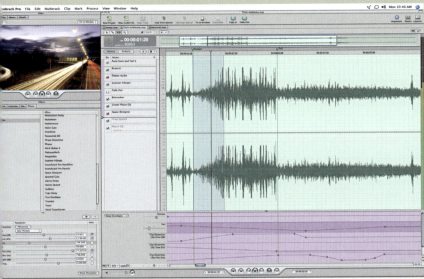

Left: Apple Soundtrack Pro
A sound editing and processing
application designed for detailed audio
work in conjunction with Final Cut.
Image courtesy of Apple.

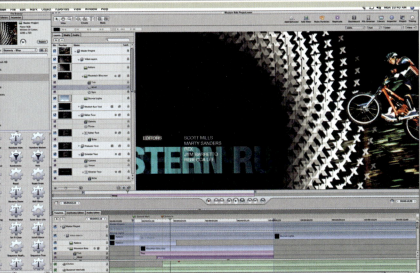

Sound from a single source is known as 'monophonic'.
The earliest disk and tape systems could only carry a
single channel of information and the sound
reproduced was therefore essentially monophonic,
regardless of how many loudspeakers were used in its
reproduction. Sound carried over two channels is often
known as 'stereophonic'. It has the potential to
provide a certain amount of spatial information and
has been the standard for music recording and
reproduction from the late 1960s until the recent
emergence of multi-channel 'surround' sound.

STEREO/MONO

The Computer

Introduction

The computer has become a part of our daily life so the virtual omnipresence of the computer in sonic arts practice is perhaps no surprise.[11] This universality is, however, potentially misleading since, although common to much of our work, the computer is by no means a factor always to be considered: it is altogether too easy to assume that because a particular technology *can* be used, that it *must* be used. There is a substantial part of sonic arts practice in which the computer has no role at all and it is important to remember this. That said, the computer remains one of the most versatile and useful of the resources that are at our disposal and, if used appropriately, can make an invaluable contribution to a wide range of practical activities.

Specialist hardware

Our computer may have a number of roles: it may act as a controller (such as a MIDI sequencer), a compositional system (using algorithmic systems), a generator of sounds (using synthesis and/or sampling software), a performance interface, a recording and editing system and so on. Clearly, the general-purpose PC will struggle to accomplish many of these activities without assistance and, in particular, those areas concerning audio hardware.

A huge range of hardware exists to meet this need and it is important to be clear about the actual requirements. For example, a system to be used primarily for recording may need multiple inputs and outputs whereas one that will be mainly used for editing and compilation may only need stereo capability. Likewise, a system

that will be mainly used to transform vinyl recordings into MP3 files demands far lower audio quality than one that will be used to produce commercial master recordings and if the system is to be used to originate high-quality 'real-world' recordings, it may well be worth paying a higher price in order to acquire an audio interface with top-quality microphone preamplifiers and analogue to digital converters (ADCs).

Straightforward sound recording, editing and reproduction does not make excessive demands upon computer power. This makes it perfectly possible to use low-end models with excellent results: the main requirements are for adequate disk space and memory. If the system will handle multiple channels, there may be a case for adding high-speed external disk drives.

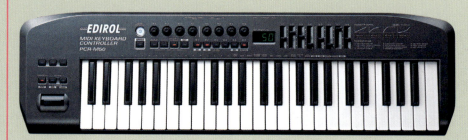

Left: Edirol keyboard/MIDI controller
Piano-style keyboard controllers are useful for entering notes on a software synthesiser.
Image courtesy of Roland Corporation, US.

Of equal importance is the monitor system. Small computer speakers are rarely adequate for serious sound work and, without high-quality monitoring, it is difficult to make precise adjustments. Headphones too require some thought, especially since low frequencies are normally felt rather than heard and headphones cannot reproduce this effect. Microphones are important too. The best quality is obtained from large condenser microphones but these require a power source. Not all audio interfaces offer this option so this may need to be taken into consideration when choosing an interface.

The keyboard and mouse is a useful general-purpose interface but, for sound work, it may be worth considering an additional controller. Especially where performance is under consideration, a

USB MIDI controller and keyboard may prove a useful and relatively inexpensive way of entering data and controlling the system. Many high-end software manufacturers offer their own dedicated controllers but these are often restricted to particular applications; in this respect at least, the cheaper units are often more flexible.

11. Commenting upon the ubiquity of the computer in his fascinating book *Electric Sound: The Past and Promise of Electronic Music* (1997, New Jersey: Prentice Hall), Joel Chadabe observes: 'Indeed, one could say that by the late 1980s the age of computer music was over because everything was computer music.'

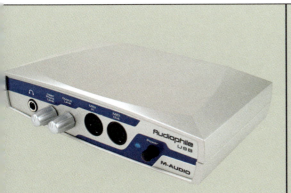

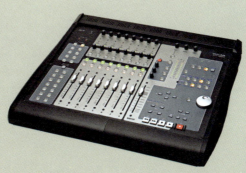

Left: Tascam workstation controller
It may be worth considering an additional controller to the general-purpose keyboard and mouse interface when working with sound.
Image courtesy of TEAC Corporation, Tokyo.

Far left: USB audio interface
A useful and relatively inexpensive way of entering data and controlling a system.
Image courtesy of M Audio.

Operating systems and software

At present, the two main platforms – Macintosh and Windows – have little to choose between them for most sound activities. Recently, applications previously unique to one or other have become cross-compatible, allowing the exchange of files between the two systems and so the choice, at present, is largely one of individual preference rather than of distinct advantage.[12]

Multitrack audio recording and mixing is one of the more demanding computer-based activities and there are many applications that cater for this at varying levels. The de facto commercial standard is Digidesign's® ProTools® system but most audio sequencers such as Logic or Cubase will carry out many of the operations for which ProTools® is intended although, almost inevitably, more slowly and with somewhat less flexibility.

A major part of such applications is the ◁﴿ 'plugin'. The ability to handle plugins is an increasingly important capability of audio software, especially since their functionality now extends to generating and manipulating sound by synthesis and sampling. Short of using a full-scale synthesis programme, this is currently perhaps the most popular approach to creating sound in the computer and has the great advantage of being tightly integrated with the recording environment of the audio sequencer.

12. Some very high-end applications such as, for example, SuperCollider, remain platform-specific but others such as MAX/MSP are now cross-compatible (subject to some relatively minor limitations).

Right: Cubase
Created by Steinberg and originally developed to control MIDI instruments, it has expanded to include audio recording and processing as well as synthesis and sampling using 'plugin' software.
Image courtesy of Steinberg.

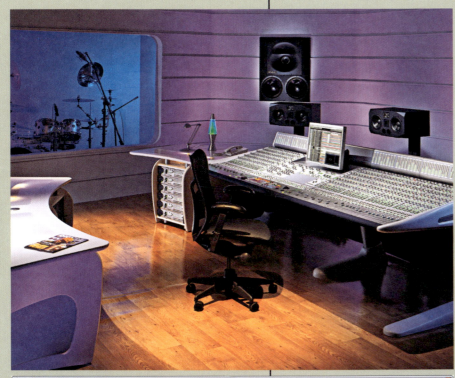

Left: Workstation controller
Digidesign® ICON workstation
controller for ProTools®.
Image © 2007 Avid Technology, Inc.
All rights reserved.

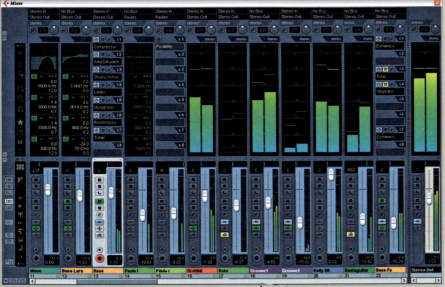

Plugins are programmes that run within a main
application and add specific functionality to it. For
example, programmes such as Cubase and
ProTools® make extensive use of plugins for
specific processes such as reverberation, dynamics
processing or sound synthesis.

PLUGINS

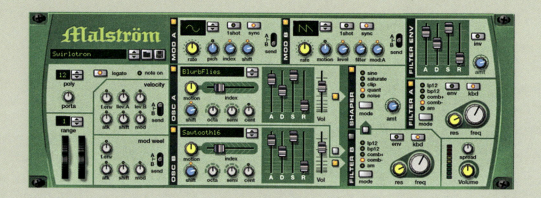

'THIS DANGER OF OVERKILL IS PARTICULARLY ACUTE WITH THE COMPUTER – PROCESSING OF SOUND AS ANYTHING AND EVERYTHING CAN BE DONE.'

TREVOR WISHART, 'AUDIBLE DESIGN'

Above: Reason
Essentially similar to, but much simpler and less extensive in its possibilities than, MAX/MSP, it provides a versatile and user-friendly resource for sound programming.

Programming

More sophisticated and flexible forms of synthesis (and other processes) are offered by dedicated applications such as Reaktor and Reason with even more programming flexibility available from environments such as MAX/MSP and SuperCollider. This, however, is only the start of work with such applications that are designed to go far beyond the sequencer plugin in terms of offering the user the opportunity to work with every conceivable sonic variable. Inevitably, this is a complex and demanding process but, as suggested above, there are several useful levels of approach to this area. Applications such as Reason create an on-screen environment that is reminiscent of the physical setup of a studio and its equipment racks, complete with jackfields, patchcords etc. and for the beginner, this can provide a useful and familiar point of entry. Beyond a certain point, however, the ability to provide a physical equivalent becomes less possible and, arguably, less useful. At this point, higher-level systems such as MAX/MSP and SuperCollider come into their own by offering advanced functionality and ultimately flexible programmability. Although sometimes difficult to master, these systems allow for a radically different approach to computer-based creative practice.

Summary

At this point, the user begins to define the nature of the technology with which she/he wishes to work rather than accepting the capabilities of a given system as a series of constraints upon what may be achieved. Here the computer genuinely starts to become a creative tool that is at the service of the artist and a vast panorama of possibilities appears before us. This exciting new landscape is, however, by no means an entirely safe place: there are many pitfalls that await the unwary. Not the least of these is the temptation to do things simply because it is suddenly possible to do them. Trevor Wishart has made a number of cautionary admonishments in his book *Audible Design*, warning that when we design or customise a system that can vary any possible parameters of a given process, we must carefully ensure that these are used in a considered and purposeful fashion. We need, in short, to make judgments and decisions that are based upon what we intend for a particular work. This is almost entirely at odds with the open-ended approach suggested by Brian Eno and deciding whereabouts along this spectrum our course of action will lie is perhaps one of the more difficult choices that we encounter in creating certain types of sonic art.

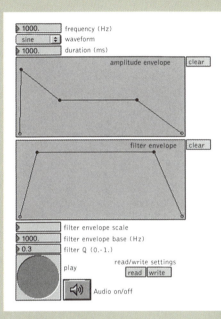

Above: MAX/MSP synthesis patch
A simple synthesiser created in Cycling '74's MAX/MSP software. On-screen objects are used to designate processes similar to those found in an analogue synthesiser (oscillators, filters etc.) and are even connected by virtual patchcords.
Image © Tony Gibbs.

Interactivity

Introduction

Interactivity is a feature common to many works of sound art. Interactive works are not uncommon in other art forms and much of what follows might be equally applicable to, for example, visual media. However, the proportion of sound work that depends upon the interaction between the artist and the system used is so substantial that interactivity has become almost a default mode for much of sonic art practice. This is not least due to the nature of the software often used to generate and transform sounds.

Much of this has the potential for high degrees of 'customisation' and is therefore useful in the pursuit of innovative sounds and ideas. In turn, this implies the greater possibility of more fully interactive operation – the temptation is almost irresistible!

Types of interactive works

Interactivity may exist at a wide range of levels, from the more-or-less unnoticeable to a full-on format in which the input of the user or participant is central to the unfolding of the work. Most commonly, interactivity involves the use of computers and software that is custom-written but, once again, this is by no means inevitably so: sophisticated interactions are quite possible without the intervention of complex, software-dependent technologies.

The images opposite show two very different installations, taken from an undergraduate degree show. They are both interactive to some extent – one using very simple audio technology and the other employing advanced and highly sophisticated custom software.

The first image of Nathaniel Mann's piece, *Foley Works – The Sound of Snow Underfoot* (2006), shows an installation work based upon the film soundtrack process known as 'Foley'. This involves the creation of background sounds (such as, amongst many other things, footsteps in snow). In Mann's work, buried microphones pick up the sounds made by the user and simply relay them back via headphones. The user hears these sounds and modifies their actions accordingly. Although essentially technically unsophisticated, the user is enabled to engage with the work on several levels and we see that what at first appears to be quite a simple work, invites users to involve themselves in thoughts and actions covering a wide scope.

The second example (by Dani Joss) uses a video camera to detect the movements of the user. This information is then used to control the generation and playback of sound into the exhibition space. By implication, the user then responds to what he/she hears and, as in the first example, modifies his/her actions.

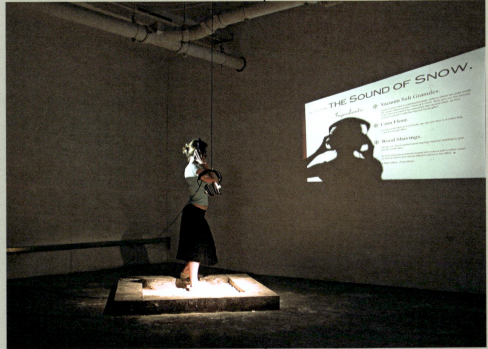

Left: 'Foley Works – The Sound of Snow Underfoot'
An interactive sound installation by Nathaniel Mann in which visitors are invited to recreate the sound of footsteps in snow using the techniques adopted by Foley artists when making film soundtracks. At a deeper level, the work recalls the occasion during the First World War when British and German soldiers left their trenches to celebrate Christmas together in the snow.
Image courtesy of Maria Militsi.

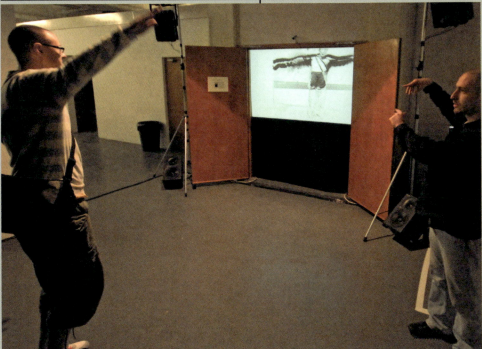

Left: 'Stasis/Kinesis' by Dani Joss
Joss describes this work thus: 'An installation that can track and analyse the motion of a viewer standing on a clearly marked "sweet spot", and use this information to influence and modulate musical composition. It features a custom sound diffusion system and video projection. As its name suggests, the central theme of this work is the stillness/motion dualism. This has been contrasted with repetition/variation and excitation/equilibrium, all abstract concepts in their own right. The installation is an attempt to move away from the culture of objects and symbolism and to revisit the aesthetic principles of abstract expressionism and the musical thought of the likes of M. Feldman through computer technology and a viewpoint inspired from the early experimentalists.'
Image courtesy of Dani Joss.

'THE PERCEPTION OF SOUND DOES NOT JUST INVOLVE THE ACT OF HEARING, BUT IS IN FACT THE PROCESS OF LISTENING. THE LISTENING SYSTEM INCLUDES TWO EARS TOGETHER WITH THE MUSCLES FOR ORIENTING THEM TO A SOURCE OF SOUND.'

JANEK SCHAEFER, 'AUDIO & IMAGE'

INTERACTIVITY

Interactive systems respond to those who encounter them. The forms of interactions may be many and varied but, most typically, the system will respond in some way to the presence or gesture (in the broadest sense of the word) of the onlooker. The viewer becomes a participant and to a certain extent influences the outcome of the work. Some theoreticians argue that all art is interactive to some degree but, in the sense that we use the term here, interaction takes place to a far greater extent than could possibly be the case if the work were to be, for example, a painting or a static sculpture. Interactive systems are often (but not inevitably) technically sophisticated and may use complicated technologies such as motion tracking – using video cameras and advanced software – or custom programmes, often created using systems such as MAX/MSP.

Concepts and definitions

So what do we actually mean by interactivity? Chris Crawford has an excellent definition:

Interaction: An iterative process of listening, thinking and speaking between two or more actors.[13]

Clearly, Crawford uses the term 'actors' in a far broader sense than normal since, by implication, he includes non-human (indeed non-biological) systems in his definition. He breaks the process down into three components: 'input' (listening), 'output' (speaking) and 'processing' (thinking). Arguably, we may wish to add another component to this list – feedback – although, in a sense, this is already implicit in his definition.

Critically, however, he points out that the process is iterative. If we move the mouse attached to our computer, we see the cursor move on the screen. We note its position and move the mouse in accordance with what we see, observe again and continue this process until the cursor comes to rest over the word that we seek. That's a very simple level of interaction involving an iterative process and a dialogue between our computer and us. Importantly, it relies very heavily upon the points of contact between us: the mouse and the on-screen display. This is the interface, one of the most significant parts of any interactive system.

Interactive systems in practice

The interface represents and shapes our knowledge of the whole system and is arguably the single most important aspect of interactivity. It has to take information from the user, convey it to the system and return the system's response back to the user. Clearly, the success of these processes is key to the success of the whole work. In order to ensure that success, one of the most important considerations is how one set of information is mapped to another.

Mapping, however, is by no means the whole picture. Allied to it is the need to consider carefully what we can and cannot constructively use to provide input to our system. One fairly obvious idea is to use the electrical activity of the brain to control our system and this has been used in biofeedback trainers that detect certain brain rhythms associated with relaxation and emit a sound to reinforce them. Similarly, systems exist for people with special needs that allow them to 'think' an on-screen cursor to a particular position but these rely on one single piece of information — the presence or absence of a particular waveform in the brain. We cannot then modulate our own brain waves to, say, increase the volume or lower the pitch of a sound. Nonetheless, in 1965, Alvin Lucier's work *Music for Solo Performer* used his brain waves as a basic sound source, which, when amplified, caused percussion

instruments placed nearby to resonate. Arguably, Lucier would have heard this and his brain activity would have been influenced as a result. The interactivity of this 'system' is, however, quite limited — it was not as if Lucier could mentally opt to 'play' one or other instrument — and so we should make a distinction between works that are truly 'interactive' as opposed to those that are really simply 'reactive'.

How can we establish what will work and what will not? A primary requirement is a source of good, clear information. If we use a video camera to track movement, we need a good, well-lit image of an object, possibly of a distinctive colour, with clearly defined edges that contrast well with the background. With this quality of data, our system has an excellent chance of identifying the object, following it and being able to apply controls to the system in response to movements before the camera. The same principles apply to any control input: the information must be as clear as possible. So, good examples might be sound/silence, dark/light, moving/static and so on. More difficult examples might be volume of sound, intensity of light and speed of movement. In other words, a binary input (off/on) is simpler and more reliable than one that varies but, clearly, it has less potential for subtlety of interaction.

13. Quoted in O'Sullivan, D. & Igoe, T. (2004) *Physical Computing*. Boston MA: Thomson Course Technology PTR.

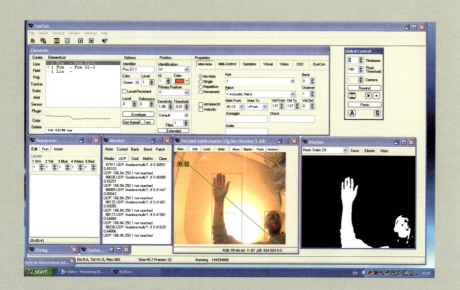

Above: EyeCon

This system uses inexpensive webcams to provide video input. The software can then track the movement of objects by their edges, colours or other criteria defined by the user. This information can then be used as a controlling input to other systems.

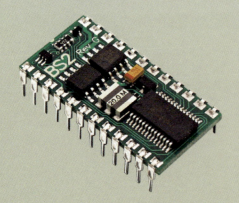

Left: Stamp microcontroller

Essentially a small computer on a single chip, the Stamp and others like it can accept inputs from almost any source(s) and translate them into data that can be accepted by computers. Alternatively, once programmed, they are able to control some systems entirely by themselves.
*Image courtesy of Parallax Inc.,
<www.parallax.com>.*

Interfaces and physical computing[14]

Once we have an idea of what form our input may take, we can consider what physical interfaces are required. Experience suggests that the design of any interface has a substantial influence on what form the dialogue with the system will take. For example, a musical keyboard will allow the user to interact with the system. However, it comes with significant cultural baggage. Using such a keyboard immediately references the Western European musical scale and so tends to impel the user's interactions in a particular direction that relates to the intervals between notes, the structure of chords, key signatures and the like. In actuality, the keyboard is merely a collection of switches (so the note middle C could be mapped, not to a musical note but to 'blue' or 'up' or 'loud' – anything in fact) but the physical presentation pushes us into a quite specific mindset that we may or may not want.

We need to carefully consider what form of input we want to offer the user. Take, for example, the idea of gesture as a controlling input. We could use the mouse for this or perhaps we could be a little less traditional and use a graphics tablet or a games controller. These all have the advantage that they plug into a USB port on a computer and have software readily available. It follows from this that devices of this nature are normally the first port of call since they offer 'plug and play' use. If, however, our needs are more complex, say in three dimensions, we may need to consider devices that are far more complex and may require specially written software. However, some established systems allow a very useful degree of flexibility but remain reasonably user-friendly. For example, the EyeCon system uses a webcam to capture a video image and track specified parts. This means that it can easily be set to provide information about gesture from the basic image and this can then interact with the rest of the system.

Sometimes, despite the wide range of off-the-shelf products, we are simply unable to acquire the technology that we need in ready-made form. This is not a cause for despair, nor should it necessarily imply a need to rethink the approach being taken. If the technology we need does not exist, it can be surprisingly easy to make it ourselves. Here we enter into the newly defined realm of physical computing. This considers novel ways of getting information into and out of computers, extending them beyond the

possibilities offered by traditional interfaces and controllers.

There are many forms of transducer that can be easily acquired (obvious examples might include infrared movement sensors and burglar alarm pressure mats) or we may even wish to go further still and build our own. Whatever we decide to use, the trick is to find an effective way of taking the information provided by the sensor and translating it into a form that our computer finds digestible.

One of the most versatile ways to do this is the so-called 'microcontroller' module. These are small-scale computers in their own right and connect to the main computer by the USB or serial ports. They can accept input from almost anything that can provide an on/off or variable voltage signal. The microcontroller needs to be programmed but this is a reasonably simple operation using software running on the main computer. Once programmed, it will often be able to function by itself although more complex systems may still need the power of the host computer to undertake more demanding tasks such as sound generation or transformation.

14. It is beyond the scope of this book to provide more than a brief outline of this subject. Interested readers should refer to *Physical Computing* by Dan O'Sullivan & Tom Igoe (Thomson Course Technology PTR, Boston MA, 2004) for a more comprehensive exploration of the subject in both theory and practice.

Interactive software

Pre-eminent in this field is David Ziccarelli's well-established programme MAX. Named after computer music pioneer Max Matthews, MAX was originally developed to work with MIDI data from electronic instruments. This is a simple, low-bandwidth form of digital data and can easily be manipulated by even a low-power computer. MAX allowed users to investigate ways of transforming this data that were not permitted by commercial sequencing or utility software and rapidly became the software of choice for experimental work in this area. Subsequently, MAX has been extended to include the generation and transformation of sound and, by the appearance of another extension, to embrace video information as well. Currently, MAX can operate upon almost any form of data that can be input into a computer making it ideal for cross-media work and it may be controlled by almost any type of input, including from the microcontrollers previously mentioned.

MAX is, of course, not the only such system; others include Pure Data and jMax. All have the same basic intention: to provide a flexible and configurable set of operational modules that can be connected in an almost infinite variety of ways to create a system that may be directly interactive or may perhaps be more self-sufficient in that it can operate by itself in accordance with a set of rules that it is given beforehand[15] or, as is often the case, a combination of both approaches.

Let's look at a particular example and the different ways in which it can be made to work:

The brief is to develop an interactive environment in which a dancer controls the generation and playing of sounds by moving within a space. We need to find ways of registering the position and movements of the dancer, using this information to control the sound generation, actually generating the sound itself and arranging for it to be played at the right time and place. Here are three different solutions:

Some years ago, this project was undertaken by covering the dance floor with a grid of burglar alarm pressure mats. Each of these was wired back to a cannibalised computer keyboard so that treading on one mat was the same as typing, say 'A', on another mat, letter 'B' etc. Each key would then trigger the playback of a particular sampled sound. This was a simple, cheap and straightforward approach, although perhaps a little limited.

A second approach was to use a microcontroller chip instead of the keyboard. This presented the data to the computer in a different form but worked in much the same way save that the computer was left with rather more power to spare which allowed it to respond in a more complex manner. Now it would consider the history of the movements and try to predict where it expected the dancer to go next. According to its conclusion, it would then send the sound out via a different loudspeaker. This solution required additional hardware and a somewhat more sophisticated level of programming.

A third approach was to use a video camera to track the motion of the dancer directly and to derive the controlling information from the image that it captured. The ability to do this consistently and reliably is a relatively recent development and still demands quite substantial computing power over and above that used for the sound side of the operation. This system had the advantage of physical simplicity (the interface was just a webcam) and gave visual feedback to the performer, thus increasing the degree of interactivity. It also provided the possibility of extension to multiple performers who could be distinguished by the colour of costume. This solution was immensely complex in terms of programming and pushed the capacity of even a fast modern computer to its limits.

Summary

We have seen that interactivity in sonic art may take a wide variety of forms and that, while it is by no means an inevitable aspect of such works, it presents opportunities that can often be too good to resist. The temptation always exists to push the limits of what is technically possible but this carries the caveat that what can be cajoled to work in the safety of the studio may fail completely when assembled in a typical exhibition space. Something that works briefly or erratically is useless in such a situation: nothing looks worse in an exhibition than a blank screen or sounds worse than a silent loudspeaker. In the case of interactive works, accessibility, simplicity and reliability are essential aspects of success.

15. Depending on the detailed form this takes, such systems are known as rule-based, generative or algorithmic systems. They may use internally created structures or may adopt mathematical processes such as the Fibonacci Series or aspects of complexity and chaos theory.

Realisation and Presentation

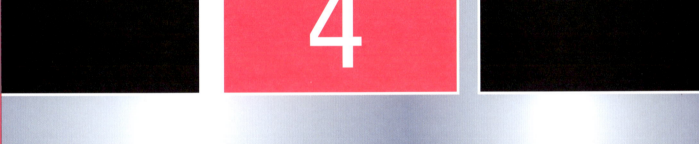

4

A major purpose of most art is its public presentation. Some artists argue that it is this that distinguishes the work of professionals from amateurs. Some go further and hold that art only comes into existence when presented to an audience – that it can only be validated by exhibition or performance. This is especially true for sonic art for several possible reasons: interactivity (a significant aspect of many works) requires participation, a substantial number of sonic artists have a background in some form of performance and, by its very nature, sound tends to be an almost unavoidably public medium. This brings with it a set of issues that the artist has to deal with when presenting work. Sonic art is not easy to present or curate by the criteria and approaches of traditional forms: it has its own unique qualities that require attention. In this section, we will consider some of these issues and ways in which they may be addressed.

Installations, Environments and Sculptures

Introduction

We have discussed the nature and relationships of sonic art, particularly with respect to music and to fine art. These definitions and relationships are clearly important as factors that directly inform the creation of works but they take on even greater significance when we come to consider the 'showing' of the finished piece. We shall consider aspects of performance in a later section so, for now, let's consider what we may call 'non-presented' works. By this we mean works that are not presented 'live' by a human agent and that generally fall outside the scope of 'simple' recordings.

Types and levels of technologies

We have already seen that sonic art often uses technology. So, arguably, might a painter depend upon the science and technology of pigment development and production. But on the whole, these factors do not have a substantial direct influence upon the ideas behind a painting or the process of its creation. Typically, the situation in sonic art is quite different with sound and computer technologies often playing a major part in the creation and presentation of the work. There is a tendency for this situation to be seen as comprehensive but this is far from true: many works use little or no 'high' technology but rely upon the properties of materials or may be activated by natural forces. Much of Max Eastley's work falls into this category, using materials such as elastic, bamboo, wood or stone and relying upon wind or heat to stir them into action (see examples of Eastley's work on pp.48–53). Equally, a substantial amount of his work relies upon electronic processes, creating a hybrid approach that uses technology as a means of presentation rather than depending upon it to help create the work itself.

In his 2003 work, *Interior Landscape*, as part of the Arts Council sponsored project 'Artists in the City',[1] Eastley created a deceptively simple installation using sand and stones brushed by a slowly moving metal arm. Concealed underneath each stone was a small contact microphone, which provided the input to a surround sound system. This system provided varying degrees of amplification and reverberation, effectively re-creating the space in which the piece was displayed (a former Methodist chapel recently converted into a Hindu temple). By continuously redefining its acoustic qualities, the piece was able to reflect upon the changes in the use of the space.

In this work, Eastley uses a fascinating combination of components from physically simple and natural materials to a sophisticated Ambisonic sound system, preserving the qualities of the materials whilst allowing them to make a far more complex statement about the space than would be possible without the intervention of technologies.

Other artists take a different approach (see, for example, the work of Dani Joss on pp.100–101), embracing high technologies and making them central components of the work. Computers often enable processes that could not otherwise be undertaken and their calculations may sometimes govern the actual creation of the work in response to a set of rules. In this approach, the artist does not directly create the art: he/she devises the rules and sets parameters within which the computer operates and it is this programme that actually creates the result.

An example of this approach is the remarkable work, *Longplayer*, by Jem Finer.[2] Installed in London, it can be heard online[3] or at several other 'listening posts' worldwide. It started operation in January 2000 and is intended to run for 1,000 years, after which it will repeat itself. *Longplayer* is essentially a computer programme that takes pre-recorded musical material and processes it so as to create a structure in which the start points of each iteration change in accordance with a simple mathematical rule.[4] From this original manifestation, Finer hopes to evolve *Longplayer* into a global radio transmission, a performable work and a mechanical instrument intended to operate for at least the 1,000-year duration of the work (see also pp.114–115).

Clearly, this demonstrates an approach to the creation of art that differs tremendously from more traditional ones. Here, the artist creates a situation in which the work can, in a very real sense, create itself and so we may reasonably say that, to some extent at least, the 'art' is in the intent. Suddenly, we find ourselves in familiar theoretical territory. The idea of intention was raised by (amongst others) Marcel Duchamp in the early twentieth century. His works included the presentation of objects such as a bicycle wheel and, most famously, a urinal, as art. This claim was defended on the basis of the importance of the intention of the artist as opposed to the specific qualities of the object itself. In *Longplayer*, Finer (unlike Duchamp) sets in motion a process that creates the work but, like Duchamp, he does not directly create the work himself: we are asked to engage with his ideas and intentions since he has no direct control over the work itself beyond designing the process and setting its parameters.

1. <www.artistsinthecity.org.uk/reading/projects/archive.asp>.

2. See <www.longplayer.org> and Finer, J., Levin, J., Eshun, K., Wertheim, C. & Wertheim, M. (eds) (2002) *Longplayer*. London: Artangel.

3. <http://longplayer.org/lp_new_site/new_listening_posts/stream.html>.

4. *Longplayer* has an algorithmic structure in that the pre-recorded sounds are 'processed' according to a specific formula (or algorithm). More details can be found on the *Longplayer* website.

This can take a vast range of forms. Some may use natural materials (such as much of the work of improvising musician and sculptor, Max Eastley, a good amount of which is activated 'naturally' – by wind and the like) whereas others may use advanced computer systems that either operate by themselves in response to pre-programmed instructions or as part of a self-generating system (one controlled by a set of rules built in to the system in advance) or which form part of interactive systems whose activities are at least partly influenced and controlled by the 'viewers' of the work.

Site-specific works

Site-specific art has become increasingly common in recent years: it refers to art works that relate to or are designed to be experienced in a specific location. They may be about a place, may reflect qualities of that place, may rely upon that place to provide input to a process or may, by their presence, contribute a new dimension to the place. By definition, however, site-specific works are hardly ever encountered in a gallery or other exhibition space. Sonic art works, particularly in interactive or ◁)) sculptural forms are often encountered in site-specific manifestations: a recent student work consisted of loudspeakers concealed in the portico of a building. From these speakers emanated a series of voices, which read the architect's specification for the construction of the building – what type of brick or roof tile was to be used and so forth, elegantly and subtly drawing attention to the built environment that surrounded the listener.

Similarly, the Eastley work discussed earlier can be regarded as site-specific since it relates directly to both the form and nature of the space in which it was exhibited and furthermore, in seeking to acoustically change the space, it reflects upon the change in the use of the space from one religious faith to another. Conversely, Finer's *Longplayer* has the potential to exist and to be experienced more-or-less anywhere and at any time during its lifetime – indeed this is arguably an essential aspect of the piece – and has no sense of site specificity at all.

Cave paintings, Roman and Greek theatres and Inca temples all provided acoustic processes that were highly specific to the location and hence the audience experience would have been conditional upon their presence at that site. These examples suggest that the location in which a work of sound art is experienced may not only have a significant impact upon the nature and quality of the experience, but may also actually become a consideration in the creation of the work itself.

Summary

By this stage, the reader will have almost certainly concluded that, if sonic art has one distinct quality, that quality is its sheer diversity. Works may be recorded, screen-based, ◁» installations, interactive systems, environments and performances of all sorts, either alone or in connection with other media and practices. In many of these forms, it borrows from established thinking and practice but, characteristically, sonic art tends subtly to subvert whatever it comes into contact with so, in the same way that sonic arts recording studio practice is different from the norm, its exhibition and public presentation are often different and innovative too. Showing and presenting sound work in a conventional gallery is unquestionably a challenging undertaking so it comes as no surprise to encounter works in unusual contexts. Creating and exploiting these contexts to their best advantage is clearly one of the most important challenges that we face and one that requires consideration at every stage of the work's creation.

'FOR ME THE HEART OF INSTALLATION ART MUST BE THE REALISATION OF "SITE-SPECIFICITY".'
JANEK SCHAEFER, '6 ELEMENTS OF INSTALLATION'

INSTALLATIONS

It is often difficult to make a meaningful distinction between sound sculptures, installations and environments. One possible distinction would be that a sculpture (sound or otherwise) implies a physical object that can be placed in a space where it is then experienced. An installation is not necessarily a physical object (it could take the form of abstract sound, for example) but is often interactive in some way, shape or form or may be engaged in an internal process of its own. An example might be Jem Finer's piece *Longplayer* which replays pre-recorded material in accordance with an algorithmic process that will take 1,000 years to complete.

Jem Finer

Jem Finer is an artist, musician and composer.

Right: 'Score for a Hole in the Ground'
In July 2005, Finer won the PRS Foundation New Music Award on the basis for his proposal to build a device that will automatically 'compose' a song of indeterminate length by harnessing the creative force of the weather. This has been realised as the work *Score for a Hole in the Ground*, and depends only on the ongoing existence of the planet and its weather systems, as drips of water 'play' the piece by striking bowls in a deep shaft. A brass horn rising from the shaft amplifies these sounds and it is hoped that the 'performance' will last for decades if not centuries or millennia.
Images courtesy of Jem Finer.

Below: 'Longplayer'
On 1 January 2000, the Finer-composed work, *Longplayer* was started; this is designed to last 1,000 years without ever repeating itself, and, though written to be played by any technology, is currently computer-generated. Finer was Artist in Residence at the Astrophysics Sub-department of the University of Oxford between October 2003 and June 2005.
Images courtesy of Jem Finer.

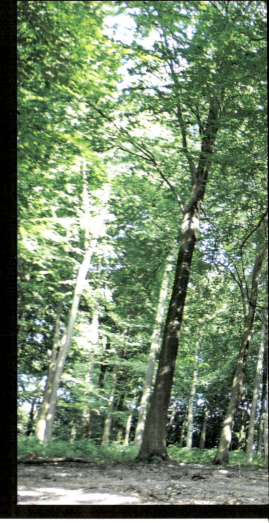

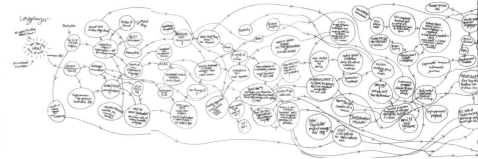

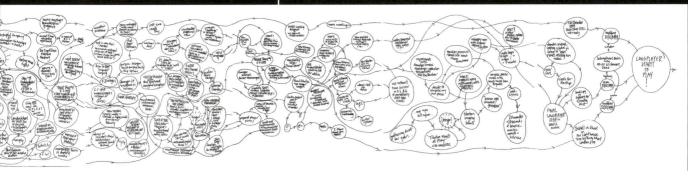

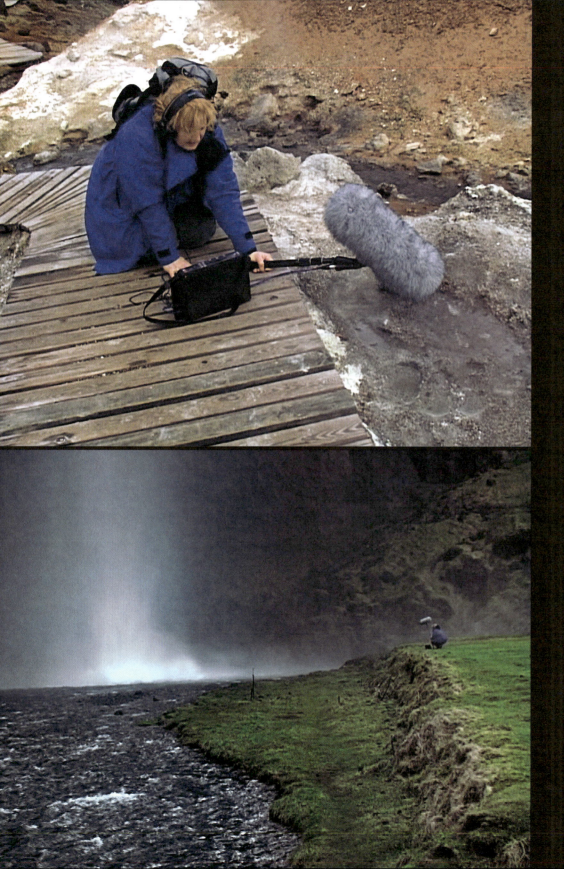

Cathy Lane

Cathy Lane has an ongoing interest in sound, memory and history which has lead to projects such as *Hidden Lives* (a multi-channel site-specific sound installation) and *The Memory Machine* (an interactive sound installation premiered at Cybersonica at the ICA, London in 2002 and further developed for the British Museum exhibition, 'The Museum of the Mind: Art and Memory in World Cultures' in 2003).

More recently, she was invited to work as a visiting artist with students in India to produce a site-specific installation exploring local history in Bangalore. She has also written and delivered papers on this area. Her previous electroacoustic music works have explored the metaphorical use of space and gesture as a compositional parameter. Other works include compositions and sound design for large-scale outdoor theatre productions, film and video soundtracks, live performance and installation work. She is currently engaged in research into live audiovisual performance and the design and development of new software tools.

This page: Cathy Lane recording in Iceland
Much of this recording trip to Iceland was spent investigating the environment in microphysiological detail and texture. Chance encounters provided unexpected material.
Images courtesy of Cathy Lane.

Right: 'Hidden Voices'

Hidden Voices is a dance performance installation created with choreographer Rosemary Butcher in 2004. The work was shortlisted for The Place Prize, London and performed at the Tate Modern and other major European venues. A film version was broadcast on Channel 4 television in the UK over four successive nights. The soundtrack for *Hidden Voices* is created largely from spoken word recordings.
Image courtesy of Cathy Lane.

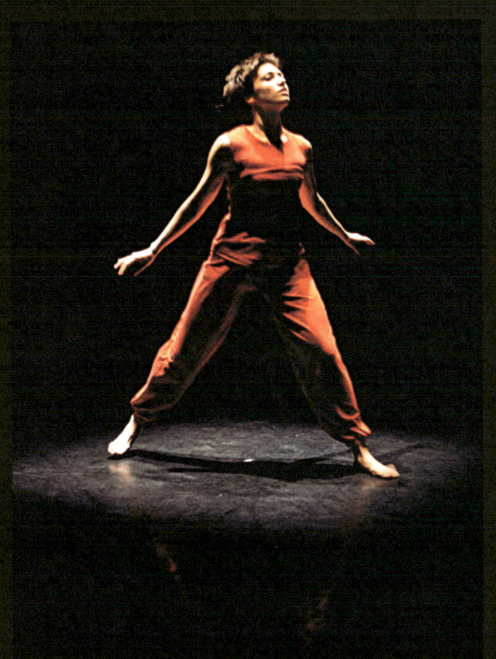

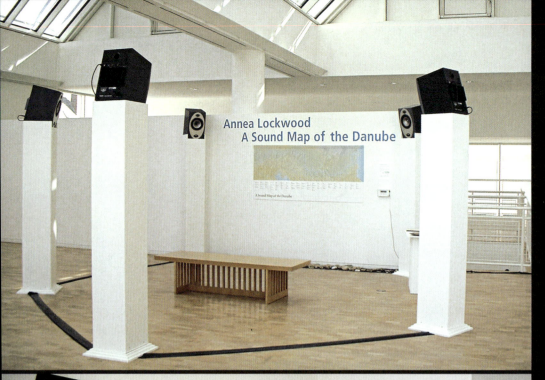

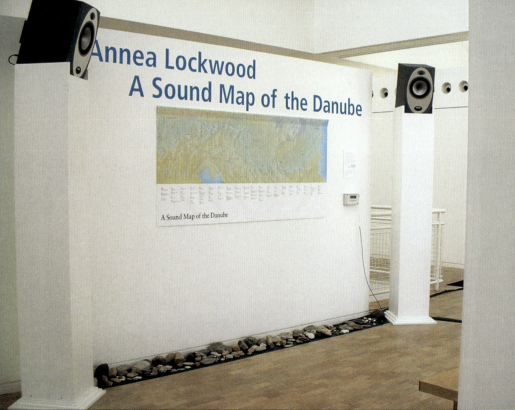

Annea Lockwood

New Zealander Annea Lockwood came to London in 1961, studying piano at the Royal College of Music and subsequently taking New Music courses at Darmstadt and studying electroacoustic music in Holland and Germany. She is currently Professor of Music at Vassar College, New York. Lockwood describes her work as exploring 'the poetic potential of sound, particularly the rich and unpredictable nature of acoustical sound' and 'blending sound with movement and images to create philosophical and sensual explorations of the natural world.'

This page: 'A Sound Map of the Danube'

This 2006 installation was presented at the Stadthaus, Ulm. It is a multi-channel sound installation with an accompanying map of the river, a time display and a tactile element – rocks taken from the riverbed, which have been shaped and incised by the river's force. Between 2001 and 2004 Lockwood travelled from the river's sources to its delta, recording the river itself (surface and underwater), and its inhabitants (human and animal), then mixed these site recordings and interviews into a three-hour work. Listeners can identify sites by correlating the time display with the map, which identifies each site and the time at which it can be heard. This is the most recent in a series of river installations Lockwood has composed since the early 1970s.
Image courtesy of Sabine Presuhn.

Right: 'Piano Transplant No.4:
Southern Exposure'
In Lockwood's 2005 work *Southern Exposure*, a little ruined grand piano was placed at the tide line on Bathers' Beach, near Fremantle, Western Australia, and left there for a week for the weather and passers-by to work on. During that week, five backpackers absconded with it briefly, thinking it abandoned; later a storm blew in from the Indian Ocean, leaving lid and legs strewn along the beach and the piano body half filled with sand and seaweed, but still producing sounds. This was the final piece in Lockwood's series, *Piano Transplants* (started in 1968).
Image courtesy of Heuchan Hobbs.

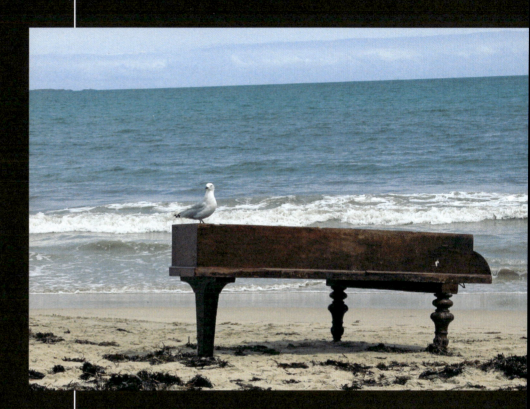

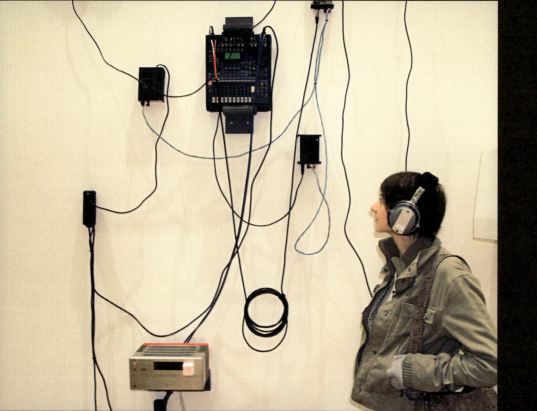

Christina Kubisch

Originally trained as a composer, Christina Kubisch describes herself as belonging to 'the first generation of sound artists' and has become well known for her installation works. She describes her work as the 'synthesis of arts – the discovery of acoustic space and the dimension of time in the visual arts on the one hand, and a redefinition of relationships between material and form on the other.'

This page and facing: 'Electrical Walks'

Electrical Walks is a cycle of works that equips the visitor with a map of potentially interesting electrical fields in the locality and an induction headset that renders these fields into sound. Thus equipped, the visitor is at liberty to explore the area in terms of the various propagations of electricity that it contains. As Kubisch says, 'With special, sensitive headphones, the acoustic perceptibility of aboveground and underground electrical currents is thereby not suppressed, but rather amplified. The palette of these noises, their timbre and volume vary from site to site and from country to country. They have one thing in common: they are ubiquitous, even where one would not expect them. Light systems, transformers, anti-theft security devices, surveillance cameras, cell phones, computers, elevators, streetcar cables, antennae, navigation systems, automated teller machines, neon advertising, electric devices, etc. create electrical fields that are as if hidden under cloaks of invisibility, but of incredible presence.'

Images courtesy of:
Left: ZKM, Karlsruhe, 2005:
ZKM, Karlsruhe.
Right above: London, 2005:
Goethe-Institut, London.
Far right, above: Bremen, 2005:
Brigitte Seinsoth.
Right: Oxford, 2005:
Janine Charles.
Far right: ZKM, Karlsruhe, 2005:
ZKM, Karlsruhe.

All images © Christina Kubisch.

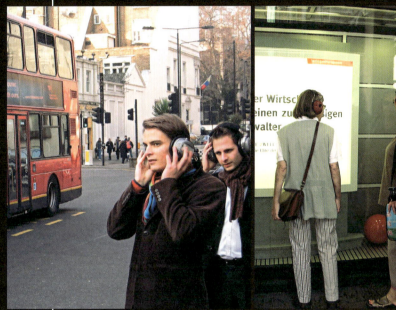

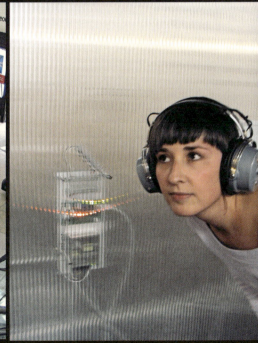

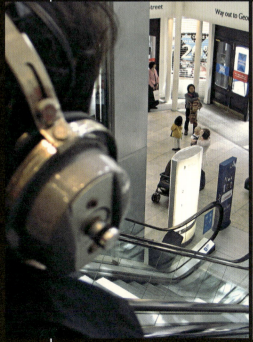

Performance

Introduction

Performance, like interactivity, is by no means an inevitable aspect of sonic art, but it is nonetheless a very common one. It exists in many forms, some of which are shared with other 'media'. Some, however, are more-or-less unique. 'Serious' electroacoustic works have traditionally been presented in the setting of the academic concert hall, often using large and complex purpose-designed sound systems. A less traditional approach often places sound performance in a quite different situation: that of the club. It follows that we are likely to encounter quite different types of material in these two environments. This is not the totality of the situation, however, since sonic art performance may also be encountered in a gallery situation – once again, the remarkable diversity of sonic art shows itself.

Laptop computers as performance instruments

The recent dramatic increase in computer power has given rise to the idea of laptop performance in which the computer has a central role in the creation of sound. There are artists who use the laptop much as analogue synthesisers were used by a previous generation: what they create is (arguably) closely related to music and hence, their activity relates to that of a performing musician although much effort is devoted to the creation and control of sonic 'texture'. As suggested previously, this is an area in which conventional musical forms have relatively little to say: a violin creates a small range of sounds and the focus of the performer is more upon articulation than changes in timbre. The sound produced by the violinist, although subtly modulated, remains indisputably that of a violin.

A performer using a synthesiser or computer works from a far broader sonic palette. We can argue that, since the synthesiser has the potential to be any instrument – real or imagined – its performer has a quite different role to that of our hypothetical violinist. Additionally, older analogue systems have an inherent instability and unpredictability so the performer does not always have ultimate detailed control over what is heard: the machine may not be in charge but it has a very substantial say in what comes out of the speakers!

TURNTABLISM

An extreme form of the work of the DJ, turntablism conventionally uses vinyl records as its source material although CDs and even MP3 sound files are increasingly used. The basic technology is that of the turntable (CD and MP3 controllers that work in the same way as turntables are also available) and the record, although sometimes both are modified. Turntablism often uses many of the basic techniques established by hip-hop DJs but extends these to include disks that have loops artificially created upon them or that may even be broken and reassembled (as in the work of Christian Marclay). Turntables and mixers may also be modified to suit particular performers.

Increasingly, these 'difficult' systems are replaced by software run on a laptop computer but, interestingly, a substantial proportion of performance software seeks to emulate the sounds of its analogue forebears: there seems to be an attractiveness associated with analogue sound that is not so commonly found with digital systems. Additionally, the laptop provides another set of possibilities unavailable elsewhere: the live remix. Much club music relies upon loops of rhythms and other components that are conventionally assembled using computer sequencers. A recent generation of software takes this idea a stage further by making it possible to undertake this process 'live'. In other words, the basic materials are stored on the computer and are recalled and reworked in the context of a performance. This takes the art of the DJ several stages beyond the possibilities of records and turntablism and allows performers to interact more directly with each component of the whole piece and to use this process as the basis of their performance; not only is the material represented in new ways but it may be re-synthesised, edited and combined in a wholly different form. The closest conventional performance comes to this is perhaps instrumental improvisation but here, the 'instrument' is the pre-recorded material held on the computer.

This is just one form of laptop performance. In others, the computer may be used essentially as a performance instrument (see, for example, the work of 242.pilots on pp.152–153), even to the extent of using conventional instrumental interfaces. Here the computer acts purely as a synthesiser and, in this mode, the performer comes closest to conventional music practice.

A third form combines the above approaches in an interesting way: real-time sound processing has only become a realistic possibility relatively recently, since it makes heavy demands upon computer power: performers may base their work not so much upon the creation of sound but upon its modification. For example, an instrumentalist may play much as usual but the sound may be digitally transformed in real time, adding another dimension to the overall sound as experienced by the audience. This begs the question of whether in this role, the computer acts as an instrument and its operator as a second performer or whether it has more the function of a specialised front-of-house mixing desk with an associated sound engineer. This debate is an interesting one, especially since it occurs in a wide variety of contexts.[5]

5. For example, the American minimalist composer Philip Glass has been in the habit of placing his mixing desk and sound engineer on stage as very much an integral member of his performing ensemble. While this predates and differs from the idea of sonic intervention using computer systems, it does much to establish the overall idea of what we might think of as performance through (or indeed upon) technology.

Alternatives to computers

Finally, we must not forget one of the original approaches to the creation of sonic art: the playing and modifying of records. The pioneering work of Pierre Schaeffer (see p.26) made considerable use of material sourced from gramophone records and also used the technology of the record player as part of his repertoire of techniques. More recently, established electroacoustic composers such as Pierre Henry have become involved in the whole idea of remixing, first as a studio process and increasingly as a live performance. The techniques of the disk jockey, once confined to the cueing or crossfading of records, have developed into a whole realm of highly sophisticated performance techniques, many of which have found their way into the work of sound artists.

Taking these early techniques as their basis, artists such as Lee 'Scratch' Perry developed the remixing techniques of ◁))'dub' in the 1960s. Although rarely used as a performance form, this established the basic idea of breaking down and reassembling pre-recorded material using audio technologies to create and control a new and revised presentation. From this came the more record-based techniques of 'scratching' and hip-hop leading to the present, highly developed forms of DJ-ing. This now has its own vocabulary and repertoire of techniques, much as any established form of performance.

All this has also led to a more radical approach to performances, derived from records, gaining considerable sway in sonic art. The work of Christian Marclay and Janek Schaefer has included revisiting material on vinyl in dramatic ways. Marclay has become known in particular for carrying out physical interventions upon the recorded material: these have included breaking and reassembling records and marking the playing surface of CDs to disturb the playback process. Schaefer is perhaps best known for the invention of a remarkable record player – the 'Triphonic Turntable' (see pp.54–61), which has three separate tone arms and can play up to three records at once – forwards or backwards – at almost any speed. These approaches allow sonic performers to completely transform existing material and present it in radically new and different forms. This idea, however, is far from new. As well as Pierre Schaeffer, many others including John Cage, the writer William Burroughs and Marcel Duchamp, have explored the possibility of the re-presentation and re-interpretation of material. To do so in the context of performance, however, has come not so much from the art community as from contemporary (club) culture and by embracing these possibilities. Once again, sonic art shows itself as having a pioneering role in a wider artistic activity.

'THE STUDIO MUST BE LIKE A LIVING THING. THE MACHINE MUST BE LIVE AND INTELLIGENT. THEN I PUT MY MIND INTO THE MACHINE BY SENDING IT THROUGH THE CONTROLS AND THE KNOBS OR INTO THE JACK PANEL. THE JACK PANEL IS THE BRAIN ITSELF, SO YOU'VE GOT TO PATCH UP THE BRAIN AND MAKE THE BRAIN A LIVING MAN, BUT THE BRAIN CAN TAKE WHAT YOU'RE SENDING INTO IT AND LIVE.'

LEE 'SCRATCH' PERRY, 'AUDIO CULTURE'

DUB

Dub is a a musical form originating in the reggae studies of the West Indies and pioneered by such artists as Lee 'Scratch' Perry and Augustus Pablo. It is characterised by the 'unmixing' of a multitrack recording such that individual tracks are presented by themselves or in small groups rather than being conventionally mixed together. These tracks are often subjected to processes such as repeat echo, spot reverberation, swept equalisation etc.

Interactivity and multimedia

So far, we have considered what we may regard as relatively conventional forms of performance: those where the artist is literally or metaphorically 'on stage' and delivers a performance to an audience. Here the medium is simple and the relationship with the audience is traditional and unambiguous. Other forms of performance exist and, unsurprisingly, sound artists are often involved in these too.

A new and radical concept of performance emerged in the 1950s and 1960s, particularly in the USA. This took the form of events ('happenings'), predominantly staged not by performers in theatres or concert halls, but by artists in galleries. Some of these blurred the distinctions between established art forms by introducing elements of performance. Works such as Joseph Beuys' *I like America and America likes me* – in which he spent several days in a room with a wild coyote – introduced elements of performance into other forms or at least demanded that the visitor become more of an audience member at a performance rather than a viewer at an exhibition.

Unsurprisingly, this re-definition of what might be embraced by the term 'performance' suits the practice of sonic art very well indeed. A number of recent sound works have involved the interaction between artist and audience becoming more of an encounter or dialogue than the presentation that is the basis of most 'conventional' performance. This results in the performance becoming, to some extent, interactive but this time at an interpersonal rather than human/machine level.

Sound as a performance medium can be remarkably un-engaging by itself. There is often a perceived need for some form of visual accompaniment, as anyone who has attended concerts of serious electroacoustic music will attest: the absence of visible performers seems to many to demand some alternative visual focus other than spinning tape reels or vibrating loudspeaker cones. It is therefore no surprise to discover that many sound performers incorporate a significant visual element in their work. This may simply act as a background to the sound or may be an important part of the actual content of the piece.

Going further, the idea of ◁ͻ laptop and other forms of electronic performance can be extended beyond sound alone. With the advent of powerful computers and specialist hardware, the idea of genuinely audiovisual performance has become readily achievable. Initially seen as an adjunct to the work of the DJ, we now see the emergence of the VJ as his/her visual equivalent, working in a similar fashion but with samples not of sound but of video and image, cutting, remixing and thereby recontextualising the original material. Going further still, we can see in the work of groups such as the international ensemble 242.pilots, an attempt to create improvised performances that combine both visual and sonic elements in a single integrated form.

4

Summary

Performance is a common activity in sonic art, in a way and to an extent that is relatively uncommon in most other art forms. Whether or to what extent this is a reflection of its relationship to music is, of course, open to discussion: some of the artists in this book would cheerfully describe themselves as musicians whereas others would refute any such connection. This raises the question of whether the way in which performance is defined in sonic art is necessarily quite the same as it is in areas such as music or dance. The range of performance forms that we encounter in sonic art is certainly unusually wide and this is perhaps one of its most attractive features, allowing it to stimulate interest and find favour amongst diverse audiences, from serious concert-goers and gallery visitors to club-goers.

'...WE CAN NO LONGER MAKE A CLEAR-CUT DISTINCTION BETWEEN THE VISUAL AND THE ACOUSTIC. THE COMPUTER WILL GUIDE US TOWARDS AN ALL-ENCOMPASSING FORM OF PERCEPTION AND CREATION THAT CLEARLY REPRESENTS BOTH THE PRESENT AND FUTURE STATES OF HUMAN CREATIVITY.'
NICOLAS SCHOFFER, 'DIGITAL & VIDEO ART'

LAPTOP PERFORMANCE

Although by no means the only technology used by sound performers, the idea of using the laptop computer as either an instrument, a processor of sound generated elsewhere, a reproducer of previously recorded material, or in other performance roles, has become widely accepted. Through the use of appropriate software, the laptop performance may take a range of forms, sometimes including video and image-based material as well as sound. Considerable debate exists as to whether or not it is appropriate to regard the laptop as an instrument in the conventional sense and whether a performer who uses it necessarily does so in the same way as a musician might use a conventional instrument.

Nick Rothwell's work covers a wide range of activities, from composition and performance to sound design, but he is perhaps most widely known for his innovative software design and programming work, which often focuses upon various forms of interaction between sound and video and performers, especially dancers. He has created soundtracks for the choreographers Aydin Teker and Richard Siegal and performed with Laurie Booth of Dance Umbrella at the Different Skies Festival in Arizona and the Institute of Contemporary Arts and the Science Museum's Dana Centre (both in London). He has also created performance systems for the Ballet Frankfurt, Vienna Volksoper and Braunarts and other projects have included work at STEIM (Studio for Electro-Instrumental Music) in Amsterdam, the interdisciplinary art centre CAMAC near Paris and ZKM (Zentrum für Kunst und Medientechnologie) at Karlsruhe, Germany.

Below: 'Triptychos'
Rothwell was commissioned by Sonic Arts Network to create *Triptychos* as part of the Cut and Splice Festival in May/June 2005. He describes *Triptychos* as 'a digital media triptych, transforming the real-time images from a video camera into an abstract graphical music score, and interpreting the score to play an interactive, algorithmic soundtrack. The panes of the triptych expose the analytical process from left to right: video capture (left), thresholding and downsampling (centre), and graphical score (right). The sound engine is a sophisticated sample manipulation instrument. Instructions from the score recall different audio selections, tunings and key intervals, and individual instrument voices play samples forwards or backwards, often changing direction and speed within a single note.'
Image courtesy of Nick Rothwell.

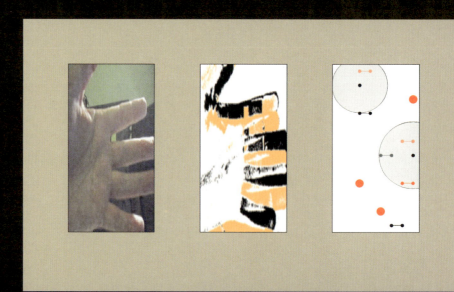

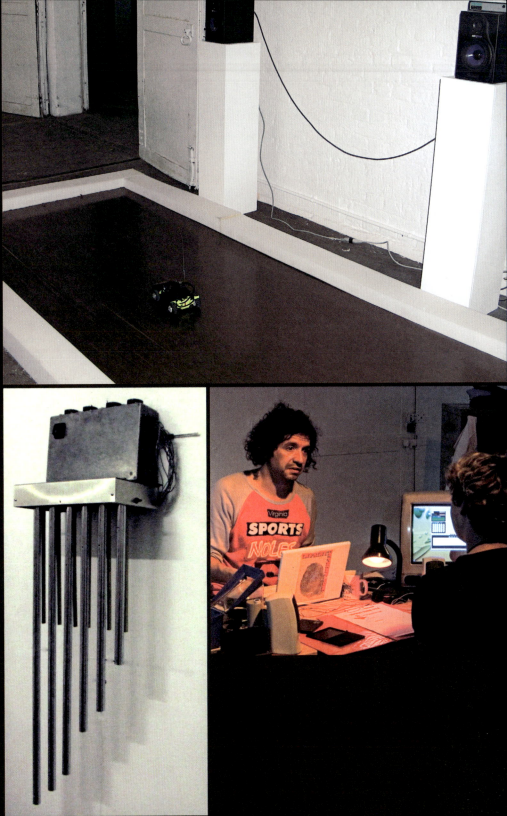

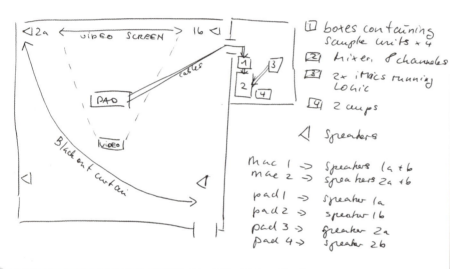

DUMPLINKS FLOORPLAN

◁2a ← VIDEO SCREEN → 1b ◁

cables

PAD

Black out curtain

VIDEO

◁

◁

[1] botes containing
sample units x 4

[2] Mixer, 8 channels

[3] 2x iMacs running
LOGIC

[4] 2 amps

◁ Speakers

mac 1 ⇒ speakers 1a + b
mac 2 ⇒ speakers 2a + b

pad 1 ⇒ speaker 1a
pad 2 ⇒ speaker 1b
pad 3 ⇒ speaker 2a
pad 4 ⇒ speaker 2b

Iris Garrelfs

Iris Garrelfs focuses upon the relationships between people and technologies in both live performances and site-specific installations. Her performances use her own voice, subjected to electronic and digital transformations, many of which are based upon the system dysfunctions better known as 'glitch-tech', which capitalise upon the shortcomings and even failings of technical systems.

This page: 'Dumplinks'
Dumplinks was created as part of the 'Sonic Recycler' event in London in 2004 and has subsequently appeared at the Arborescence Festival in Marseille and at 'Circle of Sound' in London. It is a sound-based environment created from discarded materials and recordings of sights and sounds captured at recycling facilities in London. 'Finding beauty where nobody cares to look and listen, Iris Garrelfs has created an interactive four-channel sound based environment around recycling issues, involving a found, downtrodden, but very colourful piece of plastic, and wires. Tread around and explore the sonic equivalent of a recycling plant and its constituents. Surrounded by Iris Garrelfs' multi-channel experience, rubbish takes on a new lease of life, magically transmuted.'
Images courtesy of Iris Garrelfs.

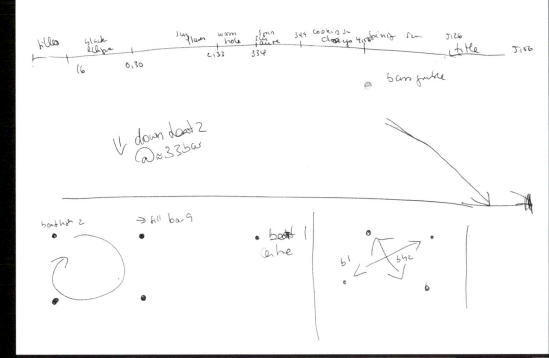

Right: 'Springtide'
Score for *Springtide*, a surround sound piece for Semiconductor's *Brilliant Noise* DVD, an award-winning solar data archive film, which will be released on FatCat Records. *Image courtesy of Iris Garrelfs.*

Right, below: 'Spoor'
Presented in 1994 in Hertogenbosch (Holland), *Spoor* was a site and situation-specific six-channel audio/photographic trail that explored aspects of urban space and also included a public talk and subsequent performance. Garrelfs describes it thus: 'I began by walking through Den Bosch, recording my impressions through photography. Images were then transformed into audio and composed into a six-channel audio installation. During this process I kept an open studio, inviting visitors to be part of the work as it progressed. On the final day of the festival I gave a talk and demonstration about *Spoor*, documenting my trail through the town and the festival, and unveiling the final piece with a closing performance.' *Image courtesy of Iris Garrelfs.*

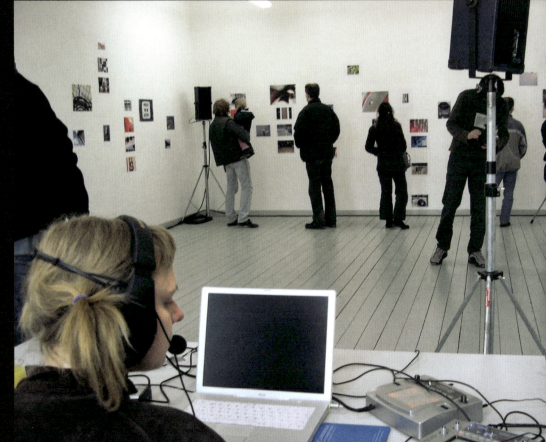

Sound Diffusion

Introduction

The practice of sound diffusion is unusual in that it is more-or-less unique to sonic art and particularly to electroacoustic music. It is also usually encountered in an academic context: concerts staged by universities often employ sound diffusion whereas performances that are similar in other respects but that take place elsewhere tend not to do so. Among the reasons for this is the potential complexity (hence cost and operational difficulty) of the sound systems involved and, perhaps more importantly, the intention and context that lies behind the presentation of the work.

Performing electroacoustic music

Electroacoustic music has, historically, been notoriously difficult to perform. This is largely due to the fact that, until relatively recently, it has been impossible for many processes to be undertaken in real time. Editing and many digital activities had to be undertaken in a studio situation and some would take hours or days to carry out. The end result would usually be a painstakingly assembled recording on tape and, although suitable for mastering to disk, it would be quite impossible to reproduce 'live' in the context of a performance.

The result of this was a situation in which the very important element of performance became, for many, a virtual impossibility. This is not to say that electroacoustic performance did not exist: on the contrary, many processes were achievable live and a number of artists and composers were able to capitalise upon this to good effect. However, there remained a substantial area of work that was simply not conventionally performable: it could only be experienced in recorded form and, for many listeners, hearing the work over the two loudspeakers of a stereo system was simply too poor an alternative to be acceptable. It was (in part at least) to fill this gap that the practice of sound diffusion was developed.

Instead of the usual two channels of amplifiers and loudspeakers of a stereo system, a sound diffusion system uses many channels (The University of Birmingham's BEAST system uses up to 32 – see p.137). The normal requirement for a sound system is that all the individual channels of amplifiers and speakers should sound as similar to each other as possible: this is not the case in a diffusion system where some may be the same but others may carry only high frequencies, others low and so on.

These systems are usually fed from a mixing desk. This can be of conventional design but is often custom-built to provide the quantity of outputs that are required to feed the large number of loudspeaker channels. The source material is often a stereo recording and the process of diffusing this into a multi-channel environment places the operator in something of a role of performer. For this reason the operator is often, in practice, the composer him/herself and the 'instrument' upon which he/she performs is the diffusion system (and, of course, the room in which the performance takes place). Clearly then, diffusion is profoundly different in many of its aspects to simply amplifying and presenting sound as would be the case with a normal PA system.

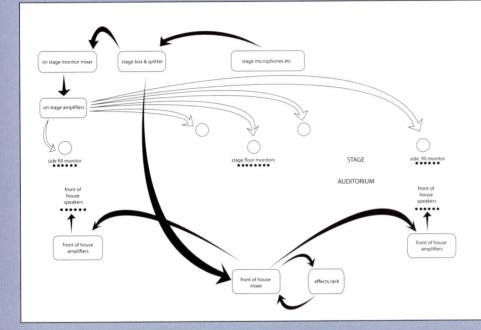

Left: Diagram of a conventional PA system
Multiple microphones (and other sound sources) are fed into a mixer which (in conjunction with outboard units) processes and combines the signals into a single mono or stereo feed which is sent to two main amplification systems usually positioned on either side of the stage. An alternative monitor mix may also be created simultaneously and fed to the performers via strategically positioned loudspeakers or earpieces.

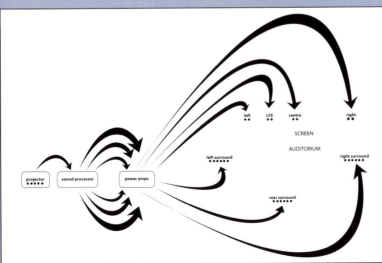

Left: Diagram of a surround sound system
A typical surround sound system, as found in a multiplex cinema. These do not attempt to create surround sound in the conventional sense since dialogue is usually sent to the centre speaker, music and atmosphere to the front left and right speakers and effects to the rear and surround units.

Approaches to diffusion

There is a substantial body of quite difficult theoretical writing about sound diffusion but little at an approachable level[6] and this may well be a significant reason why it has not been widely adopted outside academic institutions. One of the fundamental issues that theoreticians discuss is that of acousmatics. Put simply, this relates to the process of hearing and listening to a sound without reference to its source or origins. The story goes that the Greek philosopher Pythagoras was in the habit of delivering lectures to his students from behind a curtain, reasoning that, since they were unable to see the source of the words they were hearing, they would not be distracted by visual information such as physical gestures and would therefore be better able to concentrate upon those words and the ideas that they represented. From this story has developed the idea of acousmatics, defined by W. Matthew McFarlane[7] as 'sound hidden from its visual source'.

Electroacoustic music often takes sounds from the real world and subjects them to processes that transform them. One of the consequences of this is that the final sound becomes, in a sense, detached or disconnected from the object that originally created it. We could say that it takes on a life of its own that often has little to do with its origins: it has become a sound whose visual source is hidden. It is now 'acousmatic' and this means that we must accept it for what it is rather than what the object that has created it suggests that it should be. For the process of diffusion, this means that we can present the sound to our audience in a way that responds to its particular qualities and to the acoustic nature of the space in which we are working. This of course brings an element of performance into the whole process although in a very unconventional form. Now the work already exists in a complete form, rather than as an instrumental score waiting to be played. So what do we actually perform when we undertake the diffusion of a work? There are many possible answers and no definitive conclusions but John Dack offers this suggestion:

Performance is, of course, a problematic notion in electroacoustic music: it cannot be ignored by any musician involved in a medium where sounds, expressivity and source recognition seem to be permanently deferred or, at best, implied. However, if it can be demonstrated that the role of the sound diffuser (an inelegant term perhaps but one that is preferable to that of 'projectionist' – see Harrison, 1998: 125) adds something to a work's reception by the audience then can the sound diffuser be regarded as a 'performer' in an elaborated sense of this traditional term? Moreover, within the constraints indicated by a diffusion 'score' (if available) can the diffuser begin to move sounds in a free and improvisatory manner and make decisions on the spur of the moment like a 'real' performer?[8]

This seems to me to represent a sensible definition: diffusion articulates or expresses the sound (in relation to the space in which it is being heard) in much the same way as a musician articulates a previously written score: the notes are not changed but the performer brings his/her own interpretation to bear upon them just as our 'diffuser' does.

The practice of diffusion is clearly related to ideas of sound in space and these often imply multiple channels of different sounds. This may appear familiar if we remember Edgard Varèse's *Poeme Électronique*. By the definitions that we have used previously, this work encompassed a number of important aspects of sonic art: it was an installation piece, it was site-specific, it employed multiple media and, most importantly, it focussed upon the diffusion of sound into the listening space. The system that was developed for this work was substantially larger than most diffusion systems, using over 400 loudspeakers. In its time, this was a radical approach and one that, judging from the composer's own reaction,[9] had a very substantial impact indeed upon its listeners. Varèse (see also pp.30–31), however, was by no means the only pioneer who involved himself in sound diffusion. Many early works by Schaeffer and Stockhausen embraced these ideas. Indeed, Stockhausen continues to do so by manning the mixing desk himself at performances of his works, thus acting as both composer and 'performer'. This is an interesting shift of roles and one that, like so many aspects of sonic art, challenges traditional boundaries and definitions. Just as with the Philip Glass Ensemble in which the sound engineer takes the stage as an equal member of the group, so the 'diffuser' has a multi-faceted role as performer, sound engineer and, in some senses at least, (re)composer[10] in much the same way as a turntablist recomposes his/her material.

6. Denis Smalley provides this helpful definition:
'Sound diffusion is the projection and spreading of sound in an acoustic space for a group of listeners – as opposed to listening in a personal space (living room, office or studio). Another definition would be the "sonorizing" of the acoustic space and the enhancing of sound-shapes and structures in order to create a rewarding listening experience.'
Austin, L., 'Sound diffusion in composition and performance: an interview with Denis Smalley' in *Computer Music Journal* 24/2, pp.10–21, quoted in Dack, J. *Diffusion as Performance*:
<www.sonic.mdx.ac.uk/research/dackdiffusion.html>

7. From McFarlane, W. *The development of acousmatics in Montreal* (2001) eContact! 6.2 at <http://cec.concordia.ca/econtact/Quebec/McFarlane.html> accessed 22/06/06.

8. Dack, J. *Diffusion as Performance*, <www.sonic.mdx.ac.uk/research/dackdiffusion.html> accessed 22/06/06.

9. Varèse described it thus:
'It consisted of moving coloured lights, images projected on the walls of the pavilion, and music. The music was distributed by 425 loudspeakers; there were twenty amplifier combinations. It was recorded on a three-track magnetic tape that could be varied in intensity and quality. The loudspeakers were mounted in groups and in what is called "sound routes" to achieve various effects such as that of the music running around the pavilion, as well as coming from different directions, reverberations etc. For the first time, I heard my music literally projected into space.'
Quoted in Chadabe, J. (1997) *Electric Sound: The Past and Promise of Electronic Music*. New Jersey: Prentice Hall.

10. We can argue that the process of diffusion is, to some extent at least, site dependent and that the overall sound of the work will change from venue to venue. Given the enormous importance of that quality in electroacoustic works, the ability to respond to such changes could arguably amount to re-composition in some cases.

Diffusion systems in practice

There are no hard and fast rules for the design of a diffusion system. However, there are some principles shared by many: these include providing physically separate channels for high, low and full-range signals and delivering the signals to them via a mixing desk. Conventional mixing desks are often unsuitable for diffusion work since more of an 'un-mixer' is demanded by this sort of work. That is to say that there are usually only a small number of channels of information coming in to the mixer, whereas there are potentially a very large number of outgoing destinations. This reverses the conventional PA system configuration in which large numbers of signals are brought together by the mixing desk and are fed to a stereo (or even mono) amplification system.

In these examples the area over which good stereo or surround sound can be heard is very limited indeed (this is why most large PA systems run in mono). Anyone who is unduly close to a particular speaker will hear a more-or-less unbalanced sound and there is none of the sense of immersion associated with surround sound.

In the diagram on this page, we see a simple sound diffusion system in which the

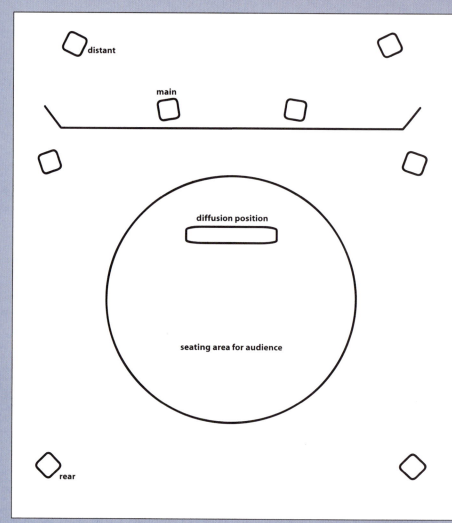

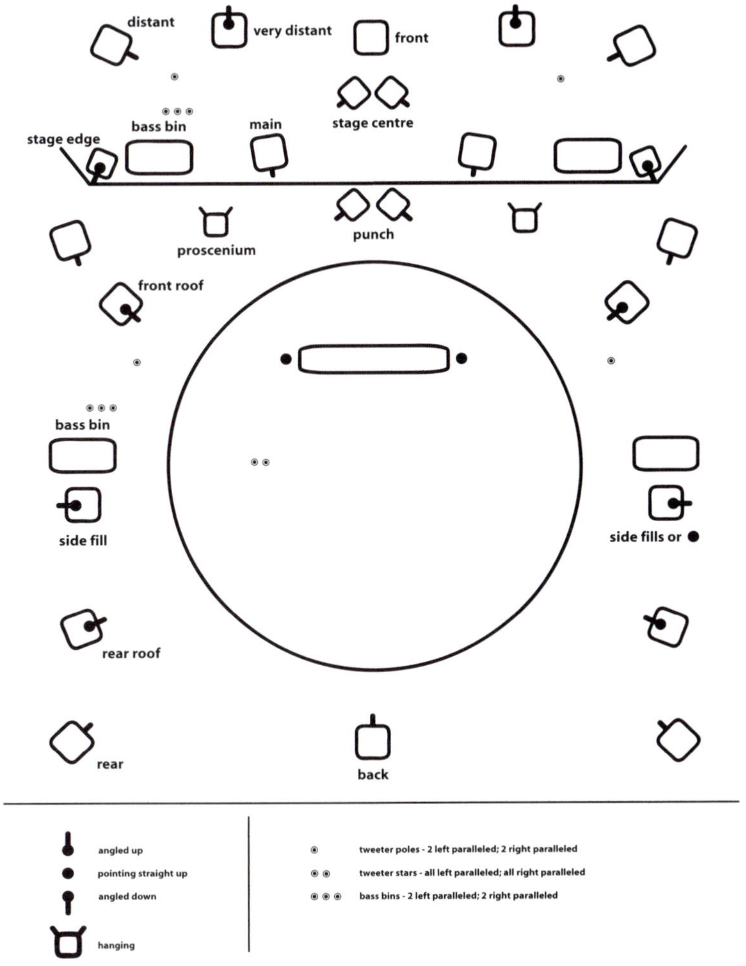

distant
very distant
front
bass bin
main
stage centre
stage edge
proscenium
punch
front roof
bass bin
side fill
side fills or ●
rear roof
rear
back

angled up
pointing straight up
angled down
hanging

tweeter poles - 2 left paralleled; 2 right paralleled
tweeter stars - all left paralleled; all right paralleled
bass bins - 2 left paralleled; 2 right paralleled

Facing page: Simple diffusion system
Using pairs of multiple stereo loudspeakers in order to create an immersive sound-space in which individual sounds can be positioned in terms of distance as well as the normal stereo space.

This page: Schematic of the **BEAST** diffusion system.
A complex and comprehensive purpose-built system for sound diffusion, using multiple channels of amplification and specialised loudspeaker systems.

main stereo speakers are quite close together with another stereo pair placed wider apart to help give emphasis to left/right differences and movements without the loss of a broad area in which a generally balanced sound can be heard. Another pair of speakers is placed further from the audience to help provide the option of a sense of greater or lesser depth and/or distance and a rear pair helps to fill out the overall sound-space. This system provides a good deal of flexibility, a large 'sweet spot' in which an accurately balanced sound can be heard; it also allows sounds to be positioned and moved around with reasonable ease. The diagram on p.137 shows the University of Birmingham's BEAST[11] system. This is probably one of the most comprehensive of its kind and totals around seven kilowatts of audio power. It features a number of full-range speakers as well as separate low and high frequency units, some hung from the ceiling or mounted high up on poles. As we might expect, the mixer that co-ordinates this array is a purpose-built unit with only 12 input channels and a total of 32 output channels. (By contrast, a typical PA system mixer might have 32 inputs but only two outputs). This is indeed a very specialised and complex system designed for very sophisticated operations.[12]

BEAST is by no means the only such system: other well-known European ones include the Acousmonium at GRM[13] in Paris and SARC[14] at Queen's University, Belfast. All these systems share the same basic idea of creating sound that envelops the listener in a way that is quite different from the listening experience provided by a conventional sound system. Similarly, anyone who has sat through a blockbusting movie presentation in a poor seat will testify to the limitations of conventional surround sound. Good though it can be, conventional surround sound offers only a very small 'sweet spot' in which sound can be heard as intended. By contrast, diffusion systems allow large audiences to have a detailed and highly controllable listening experience that goes beyond these conventional limitations.

Summary

We may reasonably ask whether these systems are only suitable for specially composed electroacoustic music. The approach taken at SARC suggests that this is not at all the case and that they may well be perfectly suited to other forms and indeed to live performance of almost any 'musical' or other sonic genre. However, such occasions are generally rare and we may conclude that the way in which we experience reproduced sound has another, previously unseen component. My suggestion is that this is essentially cultural in nature and has to do with the intention behind the work. In a sonic sense, there may well be relatively little apparent difference between a 'serious' electroacoustic composition from an academic source and an experimental piece of electronica from a non-academic one. Both may well be equally suited to being heard over a diffusion system but, by tradition, this will only happen to the former work. The latter will most likely be experienced at very high volume with exaggerated bass response on a mono or stereo sound system in a club environment. Whether this is evidence of cultural elitism or simply shows a difference in intention on the part of the composer is an argument I leave to the reader to consider.

11. BEAST: Birmingham Electroacoustic Sound Theatre.

12. A detailed description of the BEAST system and its operation is beyond the scope of this work. Interested readers are directed to a paper by BEAST's creator, Jonty Harrison: Harrison, J., 'Sound, space, sculpture: some thoughts on the "what", "how" and "why" of sound diffusion' in *Organised Sound* Vol. 3 (No.2), August 1998, or to: <http://www.music.bham.ac.uk/prospectus/whycomp.htm#beast>.

13. GRM: Groupe de Recherche Musicale: an organisation founded by Pierre Schaeffer and based at Radio France in Paris.

14. SARC: Sonic Arts Research Centre.

A practice that is more-or-less unique to electroacoustic music. It usually involves playing back pre-recorded works in the context of a performance, i.e. in venues such as a concert halls using sound systems consisting of multiple channels rather than the more conventional mono, stereo or simple surround approaches. Sound sources may be multi-channel recordings or (increasingly) outputs from computer systems and/or live instruments or may be simple stereo recordings in which bands of frequencies are split from each other and processed and played through different speaker systems located throughout the venue. Diffusion is regarded by many as a performance activity since it involves 'live' interaction with the material: indeed it's one of the very few instances of (traditionally reclusive) sound engineers becoming performers although the diffusion process is often controlled by the composer of the work in question. One of the largest and longest-established diffusion systems is Birmingham University's BEAST (Birmingham Electroacoustic Sound Theatre), set up in 1982 and using up to 30 separate channels of amplifiers and speakers.
<www.aweb.bham.ac.uk/music/ea-studios/BEAST/introduction.html>

Exhibiting

Introduction

It is often argued that it is only when work is exhibited that it becomes art – it is this process that sets it apart as the work of a professional artist and not of the weekend painter, whose work might never be seen outside the family circle. Whether or not we agree with this, the presentation of works is something that preoccupies many artists and sonic artists are no exception. The exception lies in the unusually wide range of forms that their work takes and in the technical difficulties often associated with their presentation, especially as a collection. There is no single solution to the latter issue (although, as we shall see, there are a number of useful possibilities): in the case of the former, we are presented with a range that is at least as broad as that of 'fine' art in general but one that brings with it a unique extra set of challenges. Successfully meeting these challenges is just as important in many ways as in the development and realisation of the work itself.

Forms and issues

What do we mean by exhibiting? For our purposes, I propose to take the rather contentious step of including performance within the umbrella term of 'exhibition'. Others may argue that there are a number of profound differences in the way in which both artists and audiences approach performance and that it should constitute a separate category. However, since both performance and exhibition in its more conventional sense are clearly aspects of the 'showing' of sonic art works (and it is more-or-less unique in having these aspects), I think that we may reasonably approach them together.

In looking at sound diffusion, we have considered one of the ways in which sonic art can be presented. It is one that is unique to sonic art and is unusual in that it straddles the division between performance and exhibition, forcing us to reconsider what we mean by these two apparently distinct categories. Diffusion tends to be used for the presentation of electroacoustic works that are largely or wholly pre-recorded and in which there may be no obvious performer. We then have to examine the role of the

'diffusionist' – the operator of the system – and see whether or not we should regard his/her activity as a performance although, in a sense, it could equally be seen as equivalent to the role of a visual arts curator in that it takes responsibility for the presentation of a work that has (to some extent) already been created.

So we find ourselves immediately plunged into difficulty in deciding what it is that we are presenting to our public and in what context and environment they are to experience it. If the performed work is a 'serious' electroacoustic work, it tends to be presented through diffusion (see also pp.132–139) in a concert hall whereas a laptop improvisation will tend to be experienced through a conventional PA system; probably in a club environment. The question of context then arises in a big way: both approaches carry with them a very considerable weight of cultural baggage and may make it difficult to fully understand the intentions behind the work or to evaluate its success.

When we come to consider the area of exhibition (as opposed to performance), the situation becomes a little easier. We are usually just presenting the work to the public in a more-or-less unambiguous way that derives from the established practices of other art forms and which is therefore recognisable. We might, for instance, create and present a site-specific work: this is one that responds to and/or contributes to the place in which it is exhibited. The relative uniqueness of individual local soundscapes makes sonic art very suitable indeed for this approach and many interesting examples exist.

Graeme Miller made his work *Linked* as a series of site-specific sub-works in an area of East London that has seen considerable upheaval as a result of the building of a road link to the M11 motorway. Opened in 2003 and described as 'a landmark in sound, an invisible artwork, a walk', *Linked* consists of a three-mile walk on which visitors carry portable radio receivers and visit up to 20 transmitter sites, hearing speech and music from the area and reminiscences of its former residents. This makes the visitor privy to a work that is not apparent to everyone who passes by: unlike almost all other art

forms, it has virtually no visual existence – this is a quality that is pretty much unique to sonic art.

As with Finer's *Longplayer* (see also pp.110–111), *Linked* is a work that exists entirely outside the traditional exhibiting environments of the gallery or the concert hall. The two works have this in common but, whereas *Linked* is highly connected to its location, *Longplayer* is the complete opposite since it can be experienced more or less anywhere and has little or no relationship to any location at all. There is very little equivalent to this situation in the visual arts: even films are usually viewed in a specially designed space (a cinema) and this gives us certain expectations of the work and, in turn, the space imposes demands upon visitors. The gallery situation is, of course, quite different. The typical modern 'white space' gallery seeks to impose minimally upon the visitor and to allow works to speak for themselves as far as possible. Even here, we encounter a certain amount of cultural baggage although, in fairness, this is far less of an issue than in a more traditional gallery.

ENVIRONMENT

An environment work takes an area (or volume) of space and uses sound or other media to change it in some way. In this respect, it has some of the qualities of an installation work save that the latter is usually an object that exists in a space whereas it is the space itself (and in our case, the sound of the space) that is the subject of the work. In a sense, ambient music and sound seeks to create an environment but there are also a number of works where the space itself, as it is created and defined by sound, becomes the artwork.

Problems and solutions

Unfortunately, there is another issue to be confronted: 'white space' galleries tend to be large open-plan spaces and this, together with the required bareness and absence of decor, can lead to a reverberant acoustic that is an absolute nightmare when the art makes a noise. In this environment, a badly curated exhibition of sound art becomes a blurred and incoherent cacophony that modulates only slightly from one exhibit to the next. There are ways of improving this but some have a very significant impact upon the experience that the visitor has of a given work and may go so far as to fundamentally change its nature.

The presentation of sonic art is difficult but its presentation within the context of a wider exhibition is even harder. The visitor can have exhibits visually withheld and revealed (in accordance with the curator's scheme) by simple layout and lighting design aided perhaps by a few lightweight temporary walls. Sound is not susceptible to such measures since, unlike light, it will travel anywhere that there is air or solid material through which to transmit its vibrations and the process of

diffraction means that it can go round corners too! This means that a single sound work can effectively colour the entire environment of a mixed exhibition and that it may well impact upon other works. Care and thought in layout is needed here and we may have to consider the idea of a separate isolated space as is often provided for screen-based works.

When we consider a show containing multiple works of sound art, we could logically argue that what is needed is a series of soundproof booths but, although this might provide a good acoustic solution, it would create a very strange and unnatural environment that would impact upon the works and, perhaps more critically, would be hugely expensive and difficult to create. A little common sense, however, can go a long way. Large, bare spaces tend to be reverberant but, equally, they quickly swallow up small sounds. So a small number of exhibits in a relatively large space may well avoid too much spill from one to the next, provided that they are not individually too loud or penetrating in quality. Like our visual counterparts, we can consider temporary

walls: even very simple structures of studwork and hardboard can have a useful softening effect upon sound without the need for expensive absorbent materials. Fillings of dense mineral or glass wool will help to absorb mid and high frequencies but low frequencies will penetrate almost anything: the answer may be to avoid them as much as possible and the best way to do this is not to use large loudspeakers – small loudspeakers simply do not generate low frequencies at high levels.

Possibly the best solution is to use headphones for at least some exhibits. They provide a uniquely intimate and personal listening environment and have the great advantage of spilling almost no significant amount of sound into the gallery as a whole. That said, they cannot reproduce very low frequencies since these are at least partially felt in the chest rather than being heard in the ear. However, if the requirement is to reproduce detailed and high-quality sound in what is likely to be quite a noisy environment, headphones provide an excellent solution.

Summary

Overall, there is no single recipe for a successful exhibition: a combination of approaches will usually work best. These might consist of some or all of the following:

1. Use a relatively large space for the number of works: sound obeys the inverse square law.

2. Consider dividing the space with temporary partitions: they absorb mid and high frequencies quite well but remember that, unlike light, sound can go round corners.

3. Think carefully how adjacent works will affect each other.

4. Use headphones for appropriate exhibits. Don't use large speakers.

5. Does everything have to be running at once? Stagger the operating times of exhibits.

6. Don't undertake performances when exhibitions are open: again, stagger times.

7. Use lighting to visually define exhibits: this helps to distract from sound spillage from adjacent exhibits.

'DIGITAL COMMUNICATIONS HAVE PITCHED THE IDEA OF SPACE INTO CONFUSION, SO THE RELATIONSHIP OF SOUND TO SPACE HAS BECOME AN IMMENSELY CREATIVE FIELD OF RESEARCH.'

DAVID TOOP, 'HAUNTED WEATHER'

DIFFRACTION

Diffraction is a process common to any medium that propagates by waves (e.g. light and sound). Such media can, under certain circumstances be bent, spread or subject to interference effects. In the case of sound, diffraction may result in it tending to propagate round an object (such as a wall) that, by itself, would absorb the sound if it were to travel only in a straight line.

Brown Sierra

Formed in 1998, Brown Sierra are Pia Gambardella and Paddy Collins. Their work covers a range of forms and activities including installation and performance and is characterised by their use of adapted and self-made electronic and acoustic devices to explore both the physical and emotional properties of sound.

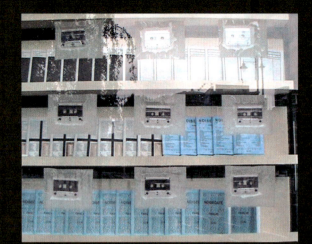

Right, above: 'Window Recorder'
Nine clear tape cassettes were attached to a shop window and left for a week to react to their surroundings in an attempt to see if anything (such as electromagnetic fields – both natural and man-made, supernatural phenomena etc.) would be recorded on them.

Right: 'Urban and Domestic Incidents – a cup of tea'
This exhibit used 180 speakers in a London flat/gallery. The speakers faced a white wall in an empty room, stripped of the paraphernalia of living. An additional wire from the electric kettle across the hall – an intervention that leads to an electronic relay via an amplifier – split the signal five ways to the speakers. The speakers were wired in five groups in sequence to the relay. As guests arrived, they were offered a cup of tea and were invited into the white room to observe the boiling kettle. The sound took three minutes to travel through the wall and speakers. After a short pause, the water began to slowly boil, increasing to a bubbling crescendo, then a click and the hissing boil fell away as it was time for tea. *Images courtesy of Brown Sierra.*

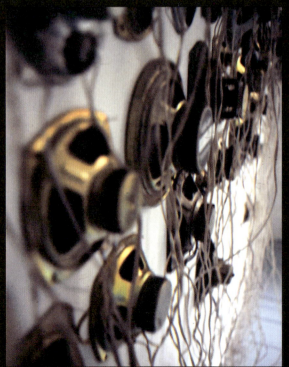

Ralf Nuhn

Ralf Nuhn, born in 1971 near Kassel, is a London- and Lille-based intermedia artist who has exhibited and performed internationally. He is currently working as a practice-based researcher at the Lansdown Centre for Electronic Arts, London, where he is also completing his PhD in Media Arts.

Right: 'Staccato Death/Life'
This 2000 work won Nuhn the prestigious Bourges Prize while still an undergraduate student.

'*Staccato Death/Life* is a sculptural collage of eleven household objects taken from the artist's kitchen, which are set into vibration by the plunger strokes of twelve electromagnets. MAX/MSP software environment hosts different, often chance-based

The underlying concept for this project was to transpose the artist's own composition and performance practice – which often evolves around collaborative projects, audience participation and the use of every-day objects as sound sources, as well as sculptural objects – into an interactive installation that invites to play, but can ultimately also perform itself.

By eliminating the necessity of a human performer, the artist intends to create a performance situation that is focused on the objects and their sonic characteristics rather than on the (musical) gestures and interpretations of a live player.'
Image courtesy of Chris Amey.

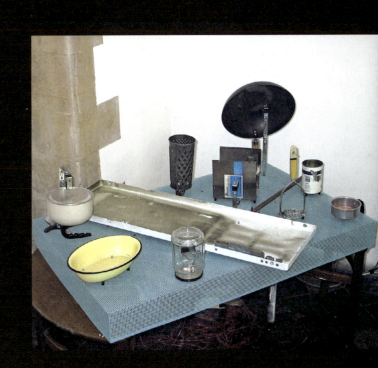

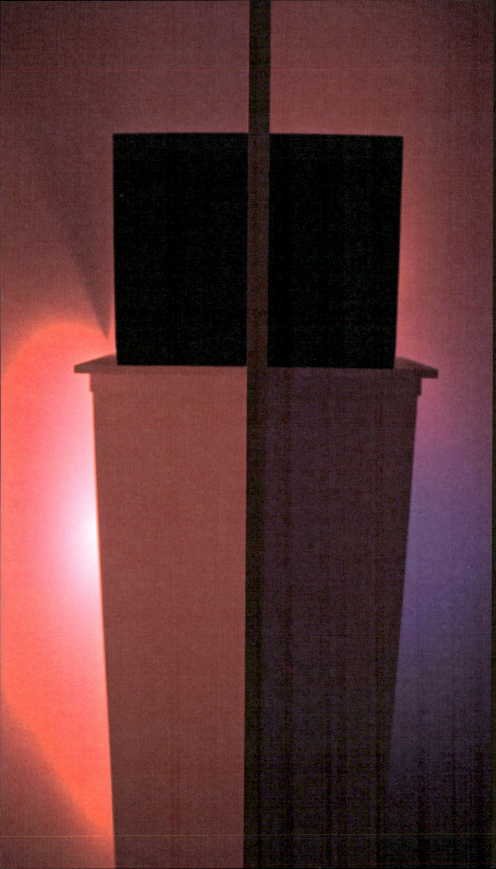

Right: 'A Question of Love'
The sound installation entitled *A Question of Love* was a community-based sound project put together as part of a larger Valentine's festival 'The Art of Love' in Kirkcaldy, Fife by Fife Council Arts Development in February 2006.

'For this piece, the process involved interviewing 170 members of the local community from primary children, college student, parents and grandparents — and anyone else who had an opinion. They were first asked their age and then the question, "What does 'love' mean to you?" Their responses were edited together into eight different age groups to make a total of approximately 10–15 minutes of audio per plinth, before repeating.

The installation space was acoustically dampened with carpeting and velvet wall panels, which also helped with the visual design. When completed, it sounded like eight people quietly talking to themselves/each other and the room was a surprisingly relaxing environment to be in. By approaching a plinth the listener could eavesdrop on the individual experiences and tales of "love". As no names were taken or given, responses were completely anonymous and were much more revealing and wide-ranging than expected at the outset. Pain and happiness were present in almost equal amounts.'
Image courtesy of Barney Strachan.

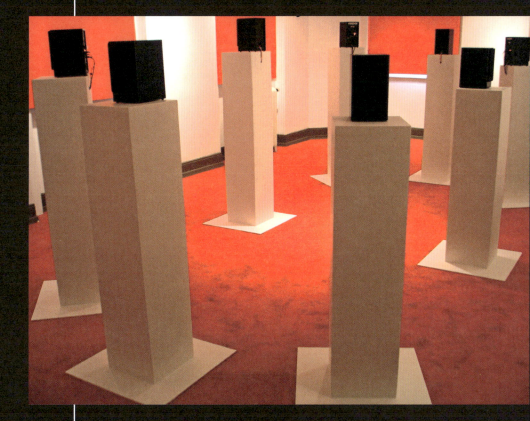

Media

Introduction

Media in various forms are important to the arts in general and to sonic art in particular. Even when they play no active part in the work itself, they are an important part of the process of preserving it for the future. To many people, this process of cataloguing and archiving is of great significance since, by implying that the work is worthy of being recorded or commented upon, it confers status and credibility. In this sense, it has a similar function to exhibiting – as discussed previously. The choice of medium for both the showing and preserving of a work is important for a number of reasons and making the right decision can often contribute significantly to the success of a work by helping to make it easily accessible to the audience. From the artists' point of view too, this is an important issue since a substantial part of their professional activity involves creating a portfolio of their works and finally, the curator must choose appropriately to ensure that the exhibition is not only enjoyable and stimulating but also that it endures and is able to be recalled for subsequent reflection and study. It is said, perhaps rightly, that a work that does not exist in at least two places (the real world and the archive) does not exist at all.

Format choice

Many sonic art works rely upon recorded information in some form and the choice of medium to carry this is important: it must be reliable, consistent and simple to use, it must be easily duplicated (to provide backup copies and for archive use), it must be in a common and durable form and it must be readily accessible by the intended audience. The choice is not always obvious since there are often several formats that are potentially suitable. Consider, for example, the huge range of video formats from miniDV to VHS, U-matic, Betacam and DVD with many variants in between and almost none of them inter-compatible. It follows from this that material for a work may have to be repeatedly copied from one format to another before it reaches the final medium.

Increasingly, the format of choice for exhibition is DVD, chosen for its comprehensive flexibility, user-friendliness, general ruggedness and reliability. Blank disks are readily and cheaply available and respectable-quality players can be affordable. The medium is small and easily portable and the format is digital and hence reasonably resistant to corruption.

Another reason often given for preferring digital to analogue is that digital recordings can be copied without loss of quality. Unfortunately this is not entirely so and DVD is a case in point, although the same problems may also occur in some other digital formats. In order to fit large amounts of data on to relatively small-capacity media, a data compression process is used. This involves the loss of a certain amount of information. When copies are made, the data is first expanded and subsequently re-compressed and a certain amount of loss of quality is inevitable in this process.

However, against this must be set the considerable advantages of DVD, which include its programmability and general versatility (the ability, for example, to carry multiple sound and vision tracks which may be remotely selected or even the option of interactively navigating through the work using choices in a non-linear fashion). Complex DVDs can be created using ordinary computers and authoring software such as Apple's DVD Studio Pro (see also pp.92–93), although the rendering process for substantial amounts of video may take a number of hours, even on the fastest computers. The result is an ideal format for exhibition purposes and one that is also very useful for archiving.

Excellent though it is, the DVD format is not always easy to programme and neither

Problems and solutions

are self-made disks always as reliable or as compatible as might be wished. DVD may have come of age but it has yet to reach the stage where, as a D-I-Y format, it is as easy to create and as reliable as, say an audio CD. The alternative to this is to have a DVD professionally made and mastered. This is a relatively expensive process and is only useful where multiple copies are to be made or sold. In this instance, it may be worthwhile considering commercial registration although, by itself, this can sometimes be a lengthy, expensive and complex process. However, it does lead to the possibility of selling the material through normal commercial outlets rather than as a 'burn-to-order'[15] cottage industry.

The issue of age is an important one for all forms of technologically based art and is a consideration for the enduring qualities of a work. This consideration comes in the form of the longevity of not only the recording medium but also of the technology itself. For example, tape-based recordings slowly but surely deteriorate as the plastic base of the tape parts company with the oxide coating carrying the recording until it becomes unplayable.[16] Early alarm stories about the CD and DVD formats appear not to have materialised so, for now at least, the optical disks that carry them seem likely to have a reasonable life expectancy. It seems that we can safeguard our recorded material but the real problem is altogether subtler. The development of technologies has been so rapid that many older works cannot now be exhibited since the technology upon which they depend no longer exists, having been supplanted by newer, more powerful systems. Any computer user of reasonably long standing will have had the experience of being unable to open an old file because the latest software update no longer supports that format and where, as in sonic arts, we may sometimes make use of fairly exotic technologies, the risk of this is even greater.[17]

15. Burn-to-order is an increasingly popular approach that, together with the use of online payment systems such as PayPal, makes it possible for many artists (Janek Schaefer is an example) to run successful 'cottage industries', making and selling their own work personally.

16. Typically, a tape recording will last around ten years without significant deterioration if kept in good conditions. It is possible to partially restore a deteriorated tape by baking it: the process takes about as long and uses roughly the same oven temperature as a meringue.

17. As an exercise, readers might like to try to track down the equipment needed to play an old digital format such as F1. This was widely used for stereo mastering and used a unique digital format recorded on videotape: not just any videotape but Betamax videotape! This meant that the necessary equipment was effectively obsolete at the time the F1 format was launched.

The Internet

The origins of the Internet lie in text-based communication for the very good reason that, in digital form, it can be represented by a very small amount of data. This means that it is easily stored and transmitted, even over poor quality, slow transmission systems. The same cannot be said of high-quality sound or video. These consume considerable amounts of bandwidth and storage space[18] and, until quite recently, were not practical propositions. The widespread availability of broadband communications, however, has made it possible to give serious consideration to the use of the Internet as a worldwide exhibition space, perhaps the ultimate in non site-specificity.

There are a number of works of digital art that have made use of this interesting concept and a goodly number of these have used sound quite intensively. The obvious example, with which we are now familiar, is *Longplayer*, which can happily sit on any number of servers anywhere in the world, all of which can, in theory, be in operation simultaneously. Hence, each version of the work is not unique as such – indeed it will be identical – but the stage of the process reached by each version will depend upon when they started so each will, at a given time, be different from every other version. This is a fascinating idea and one that finds connections in unexpected places: many works in many art forms depend upon processes that have a certain duration and relationship to those versions that precede and follow them – a Bach canon or Steve Reich tape piece might be good examples – and the nature and processes of the Internet give us the possibility of exploring many ideas of this sort.

Most readers will be familiar with the Internet as consumers but, as artists, we need to consider the practicalities from the point of view of providers. Is our work suitable for presentation upon the Web? What are its requirements? How do we set it up? None of these issues are particularly difficult at present and many companies exist to help with this – albeit at a price. A little shopping around will allow a user to buy a suitable domain name (e.g. www.tonygibbs.org) for an annual charge of around £30 and website hosting (i.e. providing space on a server connected to the Web) from around £70. The rest depends upon the artist who has to create and place appropriate material on the site. The site may be a catalogue of works or may even include the works themselves, possibly in interactive form. This is undoubtedly the most exciting situation but one that does require a good deal of technical knowledge and skill. Most importantly, however, it requires the imagination to conceive of a work that naturally and comfortably exists in the radically different world of cyberspace.

Podcasting

Podcasts are a new phenomenon but, in a sense, are really just a re-classification and renaming of existing practices. Recording material for broadcasting is not new and neither is the idea of making it into a sound file and placing it on a server for others to download: it is the combination of the two processes and the intention behind them that brings us a new and potentially exciting medium to be exploited by sonic art. But is podcasting really anything new?

We can argue that a work that is distributed as a podcast is essentially the same as a downloadable MP3 song from a website or (apart from the file format, the cover art and the physical packaging) a CD. Equally, however, we can argue that a podcast could be like a broadcast: it could be a temporary thing that is only available for a while before being succeeded by something new just as one radio programme gives way to another. This offers the possibility of creating works that are genuinely radiophonic without needing to find ways in which they can be broadcast (although, of course, we could create an Internet radio station and use so-called 'streaming' software but this can create problems of bandwidth, connection speed and server compatibility).

Podcasting has become widely accepted as a medium in its own right and is therefore ripe for exploitation for creative purposes.

Summary

Different media tend to be perceived in ways that are often quite specific to them. There is also more than a small element of 'fashionableness' which may require consideration in deciding upon the delivery medium for a work of sonic art: what attracts attention as a downloadable podcast may very well be perceived quite differently if presented as a radio broadcast. We need therefore to ask careful questions about how we see our work positioned and what we intend our audience to feel about the work as a whole, in the context in which they experience it. The answers to such questions may well inform our final choice of media.

Then there is the consideration of technology in its own right: we might reasonably think Jem Finer to be hopelessly optimistic in thinking that *Longplayer* could run for its scheduled 1,000-year duration if for no reason other than the necessary technology is unlikely to be available over such a huge timespan. As already observed, there are a number of major works of digital art that can no longer be exhibited due to the demise of their enabling technologies. The criteria for the longevity of sonic art are, in many respects, quite different from those of more traditional form and the considerations of media (in the broadest sense of the term) are very much at the heart of this issue.

18. Remember that uncompressed stereo audio amounts to around 10MB per minute, an MP3 file about 1MB per minute and a DVD containing a two-hour movie will carry around 5GB of highly compressed data.

242.pilots

242.pilots is an international trio consisting of HC Gilje, Lukasz Lysakowski and Kurt Ralske. Working with an extended form of MAX software (nato) that operates with both audio and video sources, they perform on laptop computers (see also pp.98–99) in both sound and vision. Their work is mainly improvised and, in many ways, is reminiscent of the work of 'free' jazz ensembles. They describe their work as 'a complex visual conversation: a quasi-narrative exploring degrees of abstaction, mytho-poetic elements, the nature of the sign, synaesthesia, and raw retinal delight.'

This page and facing: Stills from 242.pilots DVD, 'Live in Bruxelles' 242.pilots DVD, *Live in Bruxelles*, received the Image Award at Transmediale .03 – The International Media Art Festival in Berlin, February 2003. *Images courtesy of 242.pilots (Gilje, Ralske, Lysakowski).*

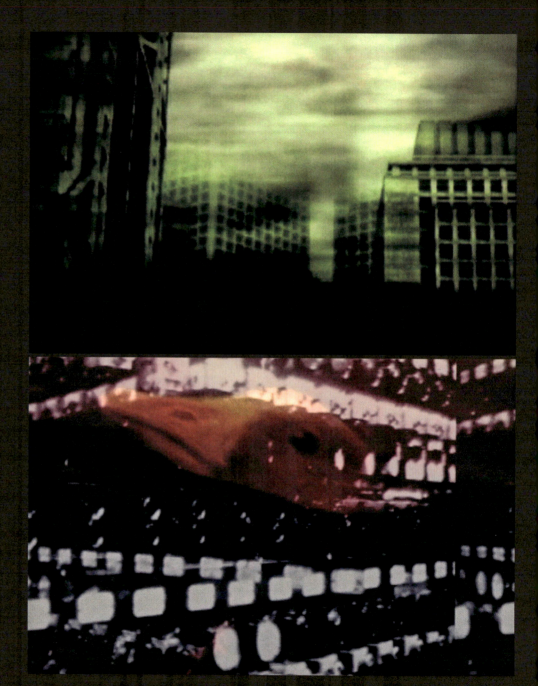

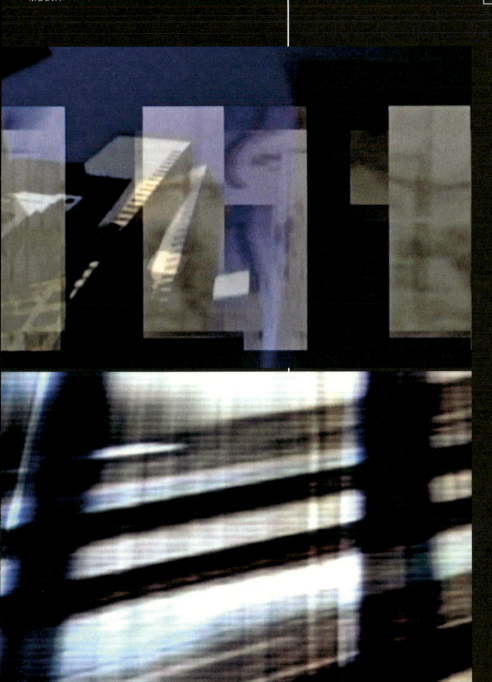

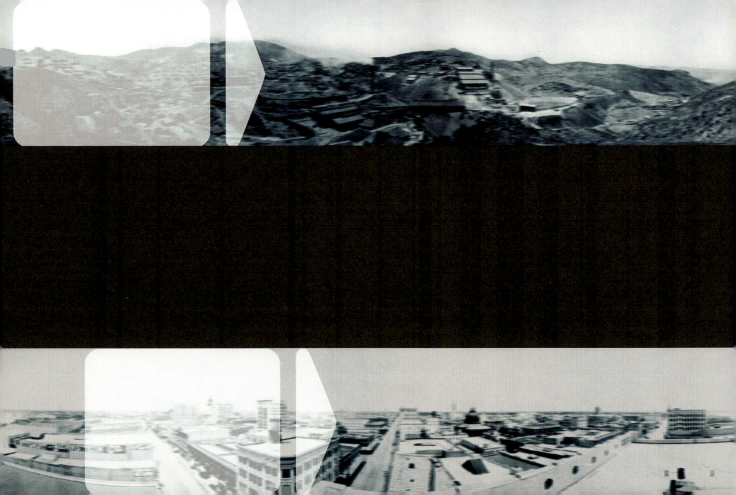

Scanner

Scanner (Robin Rimbaud) first became well known as a result of his use of intercepted cellphone conversations in live performances (his use of scanning radio receivers led to his 'stage' name). Subsequently, his work has focussed upon sounds, images and forms that are normally hidden to the listening (and watching) public. As a performer and installation artist, he uses both sound and image to create a wide range of works, from oral histories to live electronic improvisations and soundscapes.

Facing page: 'Echo Days'
A 2002 collaboration with Katarina Matiasek, exhibited in New Zealand, USA, Denmark, Australia and Spain.

'The audio environment of the installation, *Echo Days*, used decelerated and thus audible echolocation sounds of bats flying through cities and landscapes for an unsettling and stroboscopic composition. As the soundtrack entirely exists of reflected sound, it secretly transports absent structures. In the acoustic gaps of the music, the staccato image of the visible moving structures of *Echo Days* appears, their afterimages projected on to the black screen coinciding with each echolocation signal of the soundtrack. Thus edited in a mutually exclusive way, the relationship between sound and image speaks of the difficult reconstruction of any outside world by our senses.'
Images courtesy of Katarina Matiasek.

Right: 'Into the Blue'
A 2002 multimedia installation work at the Naughton Gallery, Queen's University, Belfast

'A field of balloons, as deep as the deep blue sea, engulfs the viewer, nestling up to them and creating a lighter than air environment. Soft carpet caresses your feet as you step slowly through this ever-adapting space, as warm microscopic sounds flutter around your ears. You are immersed in a new commission by London-based artist Scanner, whose work has consistently explored public and private spaces, injecting them with ideas that offer an insight into the human condition with warmth and a sense of humour. He collected responses from people in Belfast to a simple question, what does blue make you think of? The answers were then printed onto balloons that can be found all over the city and which are combined to create a multi-sensory work within the gallery. Into the Blue is contemplative, calming and a place to reflect. It is a place to touch, listen and imagine.'
Image courtesy of Scanner.

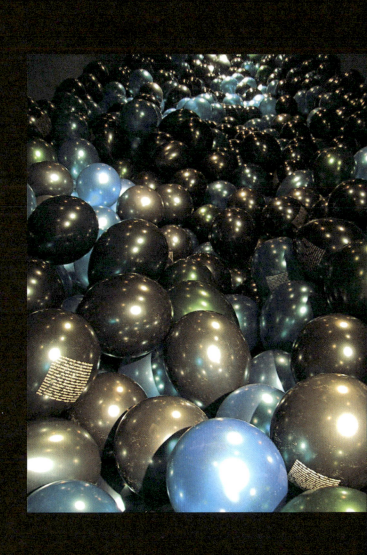

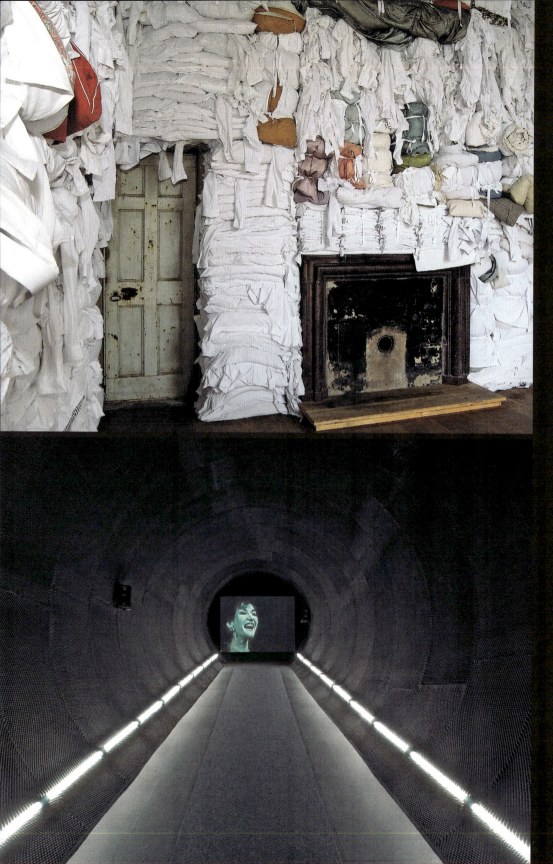

Scanner (continued)

Left: 'Belsay Hall'
Another 2004 collaboration, this time with Jerwood Prize winner Shelley Fox, this installation work formed part of the 'Fashion at Belsay Hall' exhibition (which also featured works by Paul Smith, Agent Provocateur, Stella McCartney, Jean Muir and others).
'For this commission we wanted to evoke memories of past employees and inhabitants and in some way reclaim the interior. Shelley created false walls of padded fresh white linen whilst from within this soft room can be heard fragments of stories from original staff of the Hall, drawn from the Oral History Archive.'
Image courtesy of Shelley Fox.

Left, below: 'Diva'
A 2004 collaboration with Katarina Matiasek, *Diva* appeared at the Kunsterhaus Vienna and was also shown at 'Phonorama: A Cultural History of the Voice as a Medium', in Karlsruhe, Germany.
'The voice of Maria Callas soars and cracks in a black space.
Zoom out.
The projection starts its movement with a zoom out of the black of the diva's mouth, and her lips start closing in around the yet black projection screen, her voice fading... Speed up. Accelerating from an initial slow motion, the banal magic of the documentary footage incubates the screen. The diva accepts her applause with flirtatious ease, bows and closes her eyes.
Fade to black.
From the inside of the diva the performance starts anew.
Loop.
The voice of Maria Callas soars and cracks in a black space.'
Image courtesy of ZKM.

Student works

Chris Amey

Right: 'Music for Sleeping'
An environment created using SuperCollider software through which 20 musical tones are created and presented under the control of a complex computer algorithm. The gentle and randomly shifting harmonic pattern thus created is diffused into the space via eight loudspeakers and serves as a mask for distracting extraneous noise, creating a tranquil environment in which the visitor is invited to relax on the mattresses that form the physical part of the work.
Image courtesy of Chris Amey.

Jonathan Acker

Far right: Untitled installation
Hospital infusion bottles containing saline drip on to a heated plate upon which are conductive strips that are normally insulated from each other. The conductivity of the saline forms a temporary circuit between adjacent strips. The completion of these various circuits are translated into MIDI information, which trigger the playback of recorded voices. These voices recall (amongst other things) people's experiences of being unwell, receiving medical treatment, being in hospital etc.
Image by Tony Gibbs.

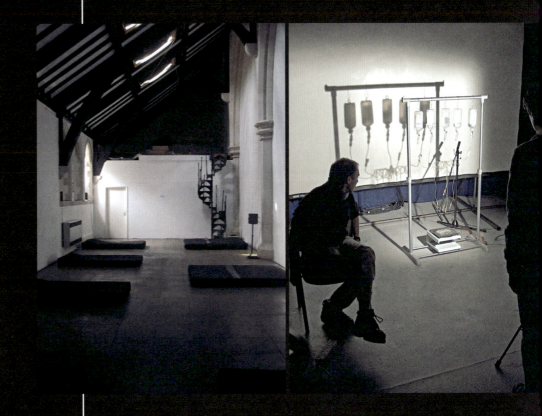

Conclusion

I hope that what you have read so far will have provided a stimulus for further exploration and discovery and even, perhaps, your own work. We have seen and discussed a number of aspects and examples of sonic art practice but obviously cannot claim these to be comprehensive. Accordingly, the following section sets out to help start interested readers on a useful pathway of study and investigation by providing suggestions for a range of informative resources.

'THE WORLD OF SOUND COMPOSITION HAS BEEN HAMPERED BY BEING CAST IN THE ROLE OF A POOR RELATION TO MORE TRADITIONAL MUSIC PRACTICE. IN PARTICULAR THE VAST BODY OF ANALYTICAL AND CRITICAL WRITINGS IN THE MUSICOLOGY OF WESTERN ART MUSIC IS STRONGLY ORIENTED TO THE STUDY OF MUSICAL TEXTS (SCORES) RATHER THAN TO A DISCIPLINE OF ACUTE AURAL AWARENESS IN ITSELF. SOUND COMPOSITION REQUIRES THE DEVELOPMENT OF BOTH NEW LISTENING AND AWARENESS SKILLS FOR THE COMPOSER AND, I WOULD SUGGEST, A NEW ANALYTICAL AND CRITICAL DISCIPLINE FOUNDED IN THE STUDY OF THE SONIC EXPERIENCE ITSELF, RATHER THAN ITS REPRESENTATION IN A TEXT. THIS NEW PARADIGM IS BEGINNING TO STRUGGLE INTO EXISTENCE AGAINST THE IMMENSE INERTIA OF RECEIVED WISDOM ABOUT "MUSICAL STRUCTURE".'

TREVOR WISHART, 'AUDIBLE DESIGN'

Afterword

Some time in 1966, my parents went out for the day. This was unusual and meant that I was at home by myself. More significantly, it meant that I had access to my father's jealously guarded 'Deccalian' gramophone and could play my new Beatles record at previously undreamed-of volume. Even more exciting was the prospect of copying it on to a newly acquired tape recorder so that I would no longer have to depend upon such opportunities to listen to 'that dreadful jungle music', as he was wont to describe it. I duly pointed my crystal microphone at the Deccalian's loudspeaker, made the ritual adjustments with the help of the 'magic eye' on the recorder and, in all innocence, set the process in motion. Reaching the end, I put the needle back to the start of the record while I rewound the tape. By chance, I restarted it part way into the recording at almost exactly the point that the record had reached. The two versions of *Taxman* played together, slightly out of sync, creating an odd spatial echo. Leaning over to retrieve the record sleeve, I brushed the tape reels as they turned, momentarily slowing the machine down.

Suddenly the world lurched sideways as the Beatles swung wildly around the space between the two machines. I had

encountered the Haas effect, one of the principles of psychoacoustics by which we perceive the origin of a sound. I began to experiment with great but uninformed enthusiasm and, later that afternoon, I found a way to combine two slightly delayed recordings of the same material and so it was that I invented phasing, the dramatic 'jet plane' effect so popular at that time. I say that I invented phasing because I had no knowledge of it before the event, any more than did the many engineers and others upon whom this honour is usually bestowed. The truth is that no one really knows who discovered it first and so I've always felt that my claim was as valid as anyone else's.

Unsurprisingly, no one else acknowledged my claim and even fewer were interested. Save, of course, my furious father who was convinced that I had hopelessly damaged his prized record player (I hadn't). For me, however, a door had opened that afternoon and offered a brief but captivating glimpse into another world, one in which a medium to which no one paid much attention suddenly leaped on to centre stage, commanding, compelling and entrancing. This was the beginning of an expedition that has lasted 40 years so far, taking me to strange and

unexpected places and forcing me to rethink time and again everything I thought I knew about sound.

It hasn't ended yet but my role now is more that of a roving ambassador between the world of sound and the world of everything else: I'm not one of the locals but I know many of them well and, having a foot in both camps, I serve as a bridge – a cultural and communications link. And so it is in that spirit that I've undertaken the writing of this book: to make the introductions, to show visitors around, to start to explain the new things they find and generally to help build links with the new sound world that so many talented and creative people have created, yet which is so little known (and even less understood) by the majority. If the people that you have met and the ideas that you have encountered in this book help to do this for you, it will have served its purpose. These are important encounters for, as Simon Emmerson says '…sonic arts is part of the soundscape and the soundscape is…the world around us'.

Suggested Reading

The following list represents just some of the many published works to which I have referred in both my research and my writing and hopefully provides a useful basis for further study. The list also includes works not specifically cited but of potential interest.

Attali, J. 1985.
Noise: The Political Economy of Music.
Minneapolis, MA: University of Minnesota Press

Borwick, J. (ed.) Various editions.
Recording Studio Practice.
Oxford: Oxford University Press

Briscoe, D. and Curtis-Bramwell, R. 1983.
The BBC Radiophonic Workshop; The First 25 Years.
London: BBC

Chadabe, J. 1997.
Electric Sound:
The Past and Promise of Electronic Music.
New Jersey: Prentice Hall

Chion, M. 1994.
Audio-Vision: Sound on Screen.
New York: Columbia University Press

Cox, C. and Warner, D. (eds) 2004.
Audio Culture: Readings in Modern Music.
New York: Continuum

Devereux, P. 2001.
Stone Age Soundtracks:
The Acoustic Archaeology of Ancient Sites.
London: Vega (Chrysalis)

Doyle, P. 2005.
Echo and Reverb: Fabricating Space in Popular Music Recording, 1900–1960.
Middletown, CT: Wesleyan University Press

Goldberg, R.L. 1979/1988/2001.
Performance Art.
London: Thames & Hudson

Harrison, C. and Wood, P. (eds) 1992.
Art in Theory 1900–2000:
An Anthology of Changing Ideas.
Oxford: Blackwell

Holmes, T. 1985/2002.
Electronic and Experimental Music:
Pioneers in Technology and Composition.
New York: Routledge

Hughes, R. 1980/1991.
The Shock of the New.
London: Thames & Hudson

Kahn, D. 1999.
Noise, Water, Meat: A History of Sound in the Arts.
Cambridge, Mass: MIT Press

Mithen, S. 2005.
The Singing Neanderthals: The Origins of Music, Language, Mind and Body.
London: Weidenfeld & Nicholson

Nicholls, D. (ed.) 2002.
The Cambridge Companion to John Cage.
Cambridge: Cambridge University Press

de Oliveira, N., Oxley, N. and Petry, M. 2003.
Installation Art in the New Millennium.
London: Thames & Hudson

O'Sullivan, D. and Igoe, T. 2004.
Physical Computing: Sensing and Controlling the Physical World with Computers.
Premier Press

Paul, C. 2003.
Digital Art.
London: Thames & Hudson

Rush, M. 1999/2005.
New Media in Art.
London: Thames & Hudson

Schafer, R.M. 1977.
The Tuning of the World.
New York: Alfred Knopf

Sonnenschein, D. 2001.
Sound Design: The Expressive Power of Music, Voice and Sound Effects in Cinema.
Studio City CA: Michael Wiese Productions

Tisdall, C. and Bozzola, A. 1997.
Futurism.
London: Thames & Hudson

Toop, D. 1995.
Ocean of Sound: Aether Talk, Ambient Sound and Imaginary Worlds.
London: Serpent's Tail

Toop, D. 1999.
Exotica: Fabricated Soundscapes in a Real World.
London: Serpent's Tail

Toop, D. 2004.
Haunted Weather: Music, Silence and Memory.
London: Serpent's Tail

Weis, E. and Belton, J. (eds) 1985.
Film Sound: Theory and Practice.
New York: Columbia University Press

Wilson, S. 2003.
Information Arts: Intersections of Art, Science and Technology.
Cambridge, Mass.: MIT Press

Wishart, T. 1996.
On Sonic Art.
New York/London: Routledge

Wishart, T. 1994.
Audible Design.
York: Orpheus the Pantomime Ltd

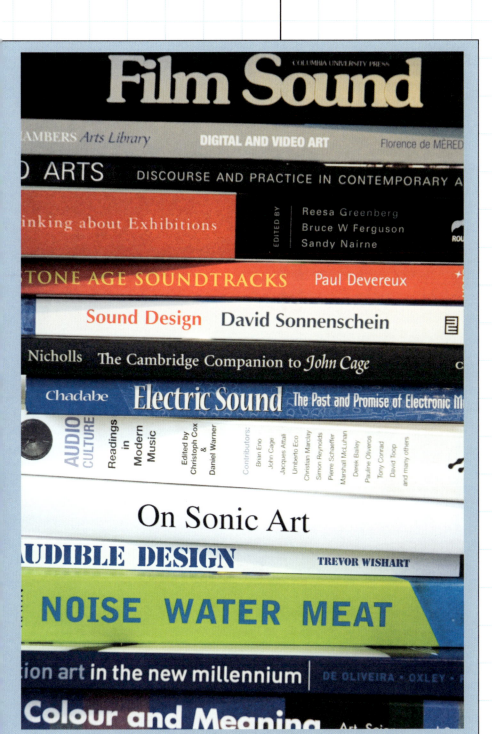

Suggested Listening

Once again, this does not claim to be a comprehensive list but contains many of the works mentioned in the text and a range of other interesting recordings that will hopefully serve to give a sense of some of the recorded aspects of experimental music that have influenced the development of sonic art as a distinct subject. Many of them also happen to be personal favourites!

Aphex Twin. 1996.
Selected ambient works.
Warp. CD 21. Audio CD

The Art of Noise. 1998.
Daft.
Ztt. ZCID Q2. Audio CD

The Beatles. 1992.
Sgt Pepper's Lonely Hearts Club Band.
Parlophone. LC0299 0777 7 64642 2 8. Audio CD

The Beatles. 1998.
Revolver.
Parlophone. LC0299 CDP 7 464412. Audio CD

Kate Bush. 2000.
Hounds of Love.
EMI. EJ 24 0384 1. Audio CD

Walter (Wendy) Carlos. 2003.
Sonic Seasonings.
East Side Digital. B00000DGXY. Audio CD

Walter (Wendy) Carlos. 2006.
Switched on Bach.
Voiceprint. B000FG4KRS. Audio CD

Brian Eno (and others). 2004.
Discreet Music.
Eg Records. B0002X7BIO. Audio CD

Brian Eno. 2004.
Ambient 1; Music for Airports.
Eg Records. B0002X7BIY. Audio CD

Brian Eno & Robert Fripp. 1994.
The Essential Fripp & Eno.
Venture. COVE920. Audio CD

Brian Eno & David Byrne. 1989.
My Life in the Bush of Ghosts.
Eg Records. EGCD 48. Audio CD

Grandmaster Flash & the Furious Five. 2006.
The Adventures of Grandmaster Flash on the Wheels of Steel.
Castle. B000ECXCAY. Audio CD

Genesis. 1994.
The Lamb lies down on Broadway.
Virgin. CGSCDX 1. Audio CD

Godley & Crème. 2000.
Consequences.
One Way. OW543634. Audio CD

Jimi Hendrix. 1997.
Are you Experienced?
MCA MCD 11608. Audio CD

Alvin Lucier. 1981.
I am sitting in a room.
Lovely Music. LCD1013. Audio CD

Alvin Lucier. 1982.
Music for solo performer.
Lovely Music. VR 1014. Audio CD

Christian Marclay, 1999.
Live improvisations.
For 4 Ears. B0000080CH. Audio CD

John Martyn. 1993.
Solid Air.
Island. IMCD 274/548147-2. Audio CD

John Martyn. 1990.
One World.
Island. IMCD 86. Audio CD

Joe Meek. 1999.
I hear a new world.
Triumph RPM. 502. Audio CD

Augustus Pablo. 2004.
King Tubby meets the rockers uptown.
Shanachie. 44019. Audio CD

The Pretty Things. 2003.
SF Sorrow.
Snapper Classics. SDPCD 109. Audio CD

Steve Reich. 1992.
Early Works.
Nonesuch. 979169. Audio CD

Steve Reich. 1990.
Different Trains.
Nonesuch. 7559-79176-2. Audio CD

Steve Reich. 1996.
City Life.
Nonesuch. 7559-79430-2. Audio CD

Steve Reich. 1999.
Reich: Remixed.
Nonesuch. 7559-79555-2. Audio CD

Terry Riley. 1994.
A Rainbow in Curved Air.
Columbia. 477849 2. Audio CD

Janek Schaefer. 2002.
Skate/Rink.
AudiOH. 11. Audio CD

R. Murray Schafer. 1972.
The Vancouver Soundscape.
Cambridge. CSR-2CD 9701. Audio CD

Raymond Scott. 2000.
Manhattan Research Inc.
Basta Records. B00004SYD6. Audio CD

Karlheinz Stockhausen.
Elektronishe Musik 1952–1960.
Stockhausen Verlag. CD3. Audio CD

Edgard Varèse. 1997.
'Poeme Électronique' on Electro Acoustic Music:
Classics.
Neuma. 450-74. Audio CD

Various artists.
OHM – early gurus of electronic music 1948–1980.
Ellipsis Arts. CD3670. Audio CD

Various artists.
Ocean of Sound. 1996.
Virgin. B0000076NZ. Audio CD

Orson Welles/Mercury Theatre Group. 2005.
War of the Worlds.
Pickwick. B000A10F4Q. Audio CD

Frank Zappa/Mothers of Invention. 2002.
We're only in it for the money.
Rykodisc. RCD 10503. Audio CD

Frank Zappa/Mothers of Invention.
Weasels ripped my flesh.
Rykodisc. RCD 10510. Audio CD

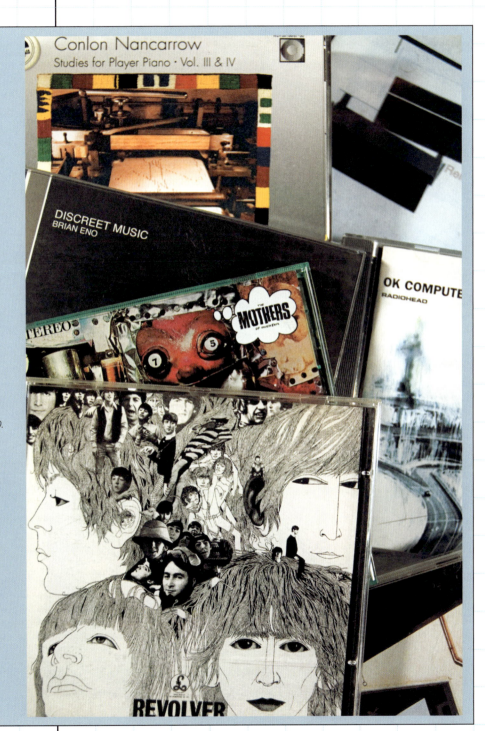

Suggested Viewing

By no means are all of the following examples
sonically significant in their totality. They are listed
here (mainly) because they are referred to in the
text or because parts thereof may be of particular
interest from a sound point of view.

242.pilots live in Bruxelles.
242.pilots.
Car Park Records. 2002

American Graffiti.
Directed by George Lucas.
UCA Catalogue. 1973

C'etait un Rendezvous.
Directed by Claude Lelouch.
Spirit Level Film. 2003

Citizen Kane.
Directed by Orson Welles.
Universal Pictures Video. 1941

Janek Schaefer - Short Stories
audioh. 2006.

Jimi Hendrix Live at Woodstock.
Directed by Michael Wadleigh, Chris Hegedus,
Erez Laufer.
Universal-Island. 2005

Jimi Plays Monterey.
Directed by D.A. Pennebaker, Chris Hegedus.
Criterion. 2006

*Pink Floyd – The making of The Dark Side of The
Moon.*
Directed by Adrien Maben.
Eagle Rock Entertainment Ltd. 2003

Pink Floyd – Live at Pompeii.
Directed by Adrien Maben.
Universal Picture Video. 1972

The Magnificent Ambersons.
Directed by Orson Welles.
Universal Pictures Video. 1942

The Pianist.
Directed by Roman Polanski.
Universal Pictures Studio. 2003

The 39 Steps.
Directed by Alfred Hitchcock.
ITV DVD. 1935

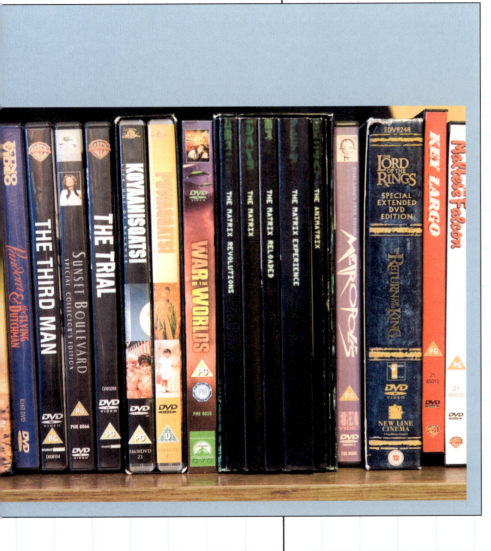

The Internet

The Internet has grown up at much the same time as sonic arts has come of age. In consequence, there is a huge amount of material to be found and many interesting dialogues to be had in the online world. However, many of these can be ephemeral and short-lived so a listing in a book can only serve as a starting point. The following list includes some of the more established online information and communication resources as well as links to individual works and artists and to equipment manufacturers, distributors and software houses.

Artists

There are a huge number of artists whose works and personal websites can be of great use. These are some personal favourites:

Bernhard Leitner
<http://www.bernhardleitner.com/en/>
Bill Fontana
<http://www.resoundings.org/>
Karlheinz Stockhausen
<http://www.stockhausen.org/>
Scanner
<http://www.scannerdot.com/sca_001.html>
Raymond Scott
<http://raymondscott.com/>
David Toop
<http://www.davidtoop.com/>
Kaffe Matthews
<http://www.annetteworks.com/>
Brian Eno
<http://music.hyperreal.org/artists/brian_eno/>
Ralf Nuhn
<http://www.telesymbiosis.com/enter.html>
Vicki Bennett
<http://www.peoplelikeus.org/>
Knut Aufermann
<http://www.mobile-radio.net/>
Janek Schaefer
<http://www.audioh.com/>
Jem Finer
<http://www.elrino.co.uk>
Nye Parry
<http://www.nyeparry.com>
David Cunningham
<http://www.stalk.net/piano/dcbio.htm>

Organisations

Once again, there are many useful organisations with substantial online resources. Here is a small sample:

Lansdown Centre for Electronic Arts
<http://www.cea.mdx.ac.uk/>
London Musicians' Collective
<http://www.l-m-c.org.uk/>
Sonic Arts Network
<http://www.sonicartsnetwork.org/>
IRCAM
<http://www.ircam.fr/?L=1>
World Soundscape Project
<http://www.sfu.ca/~truax/wsp.html>
Ars Electronica
<http://www.aec.at/en/index.asp>
Cybersalon
<http://www.cybersalon.org/>
Resonance 104.4FM
<http://www.resonancefm.com/>
GRM (Groupe de Recherche Musicale)
<http://www.ina.fr/grm/>
SARC (Sonic Arts Research Centre)
<http://www.sarc.qub.ac.uk/>

Publications

In recent years, many periodicals have begun to appear in online form. It would be impossible to list them all here. The following is a very basic list of well-established journals.

The Wire
<http://www.thewire.co.uk/>
Art Monthly
<http://www.artmonthly.co.uk/>
Organised Sound
<http://journals.cambridge.org/action/displayJournal?jid=OSO>
Leonardo
<http://www.mitpress.mit.edu/Leonardo/home.html>
Audio Media
<http://www.audiomedia.com/>
International Digital Media & Arts Journal
<http://www.idmaa.org/journal/>
Fine Art Forum
<http://www.msstate.edu/Fineart_Online/>
Diffusion
<http://www.sonicartsnetwork.org/diffusion/diffusion.htm>

Equipment and software manufacturers

Every artist's work will require different resources. Here are just some that I've found useful in the past:

Computer hardware/software:
Apple Computer (systems and software)
<http://www.apple.com/uk/>
Digidesign (ProTools®)
<http://www.digidesign.com/>
Steinberg (Cubase/Nuendo software)
<http://www.steinberg.net/>
Propellerheads (Reason software)
<http://www.propellerheads.se/>
Cycling74 (MAX/MSP software)
<http://www.cycling74.com>
Native Instruments (REAKTOR software)
<http://www.native-instruments.com>
SuperCollider (software)
<http://sourceforge.net/project/showfiles.php?group_id=54622>

Electronics:
Making Things (interactive electronics)
<http://www.makingthings.com/>
Maplin Electronics (electronic components)
<http://www.maplin.co.uk>

Audio and studio hardware:
HHB Communications (pro-audio systems)
<http://www.hhb.co.uk/>
Behringer (audio hardware)
<http://www.behringer.com/>
Boss (Roland) (audio/music hardware)
<http://www.roland.co.uk>
Studiospares (studio miscellaneous)
<http://www.studiospares.com>

Glossary

Acousmatic
A sound that has no apparent visual origin or that is heard in isolation from its source.

Acoustics
The qualities of a space that, by modifying a sound, have an impact upon its qualities or the way in which it is experienced.

A/D converter
The electronic means whereby an audio signal is converted into digital form (and vice versa).

Algorithm
A formula or a closely defined procedure. Specialist algorithms can be used to create and transform sound within computers. An algorithm applies a particular (usually numerical) process to incoming data resulting in that data being changed in a more-or-less predictable fashion.

Convolution
1) The recreation of the acoustic qualities of a space.
2) The merging of two different sounds using a computer.

Delay
The insertion of a time lag before a sound is re-heard. Usually achieved by means of a digital delay line.

Diffusion
1) The way in which different frequencies are affected by acoustic or reverberant factors.
2) A practice characteristic of electroacoustic performance using multiple loudspeakers.

Dynamics
The qualities of a sound that are defined by its volume at a given instant or instants.

Echo
A sound repeatedly delayed and replayed, typically with each repeat quieter than the one before.

Envelope
The overall dynamic qualities of a sound – normally defined in terms of attack, decay, sustain, release.

Environment
Artwork that seeks to modulate the immediate surroundings by means of sound and/or visual projections rather than by the display of specific objects.

Feedback
Connecting the output of a process back to the input, either in order to be reprocessed or to apply a controlling influence.

Filter
An electronic device that can selectively control the level of different frequency components of a sound.

Granulation
The manipulation of sound whereby the sound is not directly created from scratch nor is an existing sound sampled in the normal sense of the word. Instead, an existing sound is dissected into very short 'grains' (typically less than 50ms long) each of which can then be manipulated, superimposed and reproduced at will.

Harmonic
A single frequency component of a complex sound.

Interactivity
A two-way relationship in which a process is influenced by someone (or thing) and which, in turn, influences the responses of that person (or thing).

Interface
The mediating structure between a system and the person using it.

Iteration
A repeated process whereby the output of a system is (normally) fed back to the input to be processed a second (and subsequent) time/s.

Microcontroller
A one-chip computer frequently used to derive input to and create output from interactive systems.

MIDI
Musical Instrument Digital Interface – a digital signal system designed originally to allow electronic instruments to communicate with each other. Now extensively used to communicate between computers and external hardware.

Mixdown
The process of combining the multiple signals recorded by a multitrack system. It may involve modifications and processing of sounds and their placement in a mono, stereo or surround sound environment. Also known as 'reduction'.

Mixer
An electronic system for combining multiple audio signals.

Multitrack
A recording system capable of accepting and reproducing multiple inputs simultaneously and separately.

Noise gate
An audio processor which only passes a signal when its volume exceeds a predetermined level.

Overdub
A recording process using multitrack systems in which a second (or subsequent) layer is added (usually separately) to an existing recording.

Preamp(lifier)
A circuit, which amplifies a small electrical signal (e.g. from a microphone) to a higher amplitude to facilitate subsequent processing and amplification.

Radiophonics
Originally, specialist sound designed for use in radio programmes. Increasingly applied to sound works designed to be heard in isolation or which have a narrative quality.

Readymade
Term coined by Marcel Duchamp to describe the practice of exhibiting pre-existing (and often everyday) objects as art.

Reduction
See mixdown.

Reverberation
The way in which a sound dies away in a real or virtual space. Normally defined as the time it takes for the sound to die down to one millionth of its original volume.

Sampler
A system (hardware or software) designed to allow real-world sounds to be processed and treated in the same way as those generated by a synthesiser.

Sequencer
A system (hardware or software) designed to allow the recording, editing and playback of information (audio and/or MIDI).

Serialism
An alternative to the traditional structure of chords and intervals usually referred to as tonality, its uses widened by later composers to include the structuring of time, dynamics and timbre within orchestral composition.

Sine wave
A pure sound of a single pitch with no harmonics.

Square wave
A pitched sound, very rich in harmonics.

Synthesiser
A system (hardware or software) designed to allow the flexible creation of sound from basic sources (e.g. oscillators) by means of processes such as filtering and enveloping.

Transducer
A means of turning information in one form into another (e.g. a microphone turns sound as vibrations in air into an electrical signal).

Vocoder
A system (hardware or software) that imposes the energy distribution of one sound (the modulator) on to another (the carrier).

White noise
Broadband noise made up of a largely random collection of frequencies. A very rich potential sound source.

White space
A gallery characterised by absence of decorative features and (usually) white walls and ceilings designed to have as little impact as possible upon the work being shown.

Index

242.pilots 126, 152–3

Acker, Jonathan 157
acousmatics 134
acoustics 14, 20, 24
ambient music 18, 38, 39
Amey, Chris 157
amplified sound 49
analytical approach 86–9
ancient cultures 14, 20
architecture 20–1, 37, 48–9, 54–5
art forms
  defining 8, 36, 43, 53
  developments 32–3
  technology relationship 13
  see also fine art; sonic art
Art of Noises manifesto 15, 22–3
articulation 80–3
artists' websites 168
audiences 45, 55, 61, 86, 109
audio hardware manufacturers 169
Aufermann, Knut 66–71

Bacon, Francis 14, 21, 29
BEAST diffusion system 132, 137–8
Bennett, Vicki 44–7
broadcasting 38
  see also radio...
Brown Sierra 144

Cage, John 10, 16–17, 19, 34–5
Cape Farewell project 48–9
chance 34
composer's role 32, 37, 64
computer technology 17–18, 29, 94–107, 122–3,
126–7, 169
controllers 95, 97, 104–7
convolution systems 84

delay systems 74–9
design, defining 36
  see also sound design
diffraction 142, 143
diffusion systems 132–40
digital technology 61, 79, 148–51
DJ-ing 35, 122–4

dub 124, 125
Duchamp, Marcel 34, 111
DVD format 148–9
dynamics processors 80–3

Eastley, Max 48–53, 110, 112
editing programmes 86–7, 92–3, 94
electroacoustic music 26–9, 53, 62–4, 132, 138–9
electronic music 26, 27
electronics 24–5, 169
Emmerson, Simon 62–5
Eno, Brian 18, 33, 38–9, 78–9
environments 110–21, 141
exhibiting work 109, 140–7
experimental music 32–3, 64, 69, 71, 164–5

feedback 67–70, 74–9
film sound 25, 36–8, 90–2, 166
fine art 41, 43
  see also art forms
Finer, Jem 111–12, 113–15, 141
Foley Works 100–1
Fox, Shelley 156
Fripp, Robert 77–8
Furness, Patrick 129

gallery spaces 141–2
Garrelfs, Iris 130–1
gate 80, 82
Greek culture 14, 20

hardware 94–5, 169
headphones 95, 142
Hendrix, Jimi 76–7, 84
historical perspective 14–29
Horn, Trevor 23
hyperinstruments 76, 77

installations 42, 48–55, 60, 100–1, 110–21
interactivity 32–3, 100–7, 109, 126
interfaces 95, 104–5
Internet 150, 168–9
iteration 74–9

Jeck, Philip 55, 60
Joss, Dani 100–1, 110–11

keyboards 94–5, 104
kinetic art 48–53
Kubisch, Christina 120–1

Lane, Cathy 116–17
laptop performances 122–3, 126–7
LMC see London Musicians Collective
location recording 84, 86, 88
Lockwood, Annea 118–19
London Musicians Collective (LMC) 69
Lucier, Alvin 103

Mann, Nathaniel 100–1
Marclay, Christian 124
Matiasek, Katarina 155, 156
MAX 106
media 148–57
microcontrollers 104, 105, 106–7
microphones 24–5, 95
Miller, Graeme 141
minimalism 32, 64
mixing desks 132–9
monitor systems 95
monophonic sound 92, 93
multimedia performances 126
multitrack systems 96
music
  Art of Noises manifesto 23
  artists' use 48–9, 53, 55, 62–5, 69, 71
  developments 32–5
  sonic art relationship 9, 30, 41, 43
  suggested listening 164–5
  see also electroacoustic music
  Musique Concrète 14, 26, 43

noise gate 80, 82
Nuhn, Ralf 145

operating systems 96–7

PA systems 132–3, 136
Paik, Nam June 33, 34
Pavlatos, Johnny 129
People Like Us 44–7
performance 69, 109, 122–32, 138–40
phasing 161

physical computing 104–5
Pigrem, Jonathan 129
place and space 84
plugins 96–7
podcasting 38, 71, 151
popular music 63–4
presenting work 109–57
programming 99
psychoacoustics 38, 161
public awareness 61, 63, 71
  see also presenting work
publications 162, 169

radio stations 66–71
Radiophonic Workshop 19, 26
radiophonics 24, 25, 38
Reaktor 88–9
Reason 98–9
record players 54–7, 59–61, 124
recording systems 14–16, 24–6, 28–9
  artists' use 49, 53
  hardware 94
  studio practice 74–85
  synthesis 86, 88
Reich, Steve 17, 32–3, 77
Resonance104.4fm 66–7, 69–71
reverberation systems 83–4
Riley, Terry 77
Rimbaud, Robin 154–6
Roman culture 14, 20
Rothwell, Nick 128
Russolo, Luigi 15, 22–3

Scanner 154–6
Schaefer, Janek 42, 54–61, 124
Schaeffer, Pierre 16, 26–7, 30, 124
Scott, Raymond 26
sculptures 48, 51–2, 110–21
site-specific works 42, 112
  see also installations
software 83, 88–9, 96–7, 100, 106–7, 169
sonic art
  defining 8–9, 60, 63–4
  forms 11
sound
  articulation 80–3

creating 86–93
  diffusion 132–40
  pre-electricity 20–1
  role in art 8, 11, 34
sound design
  defining 9, 36, 60
  practice 36–8, 86–93
sound sculpture 112
  see also sculptures
soundscaping 28, 64
space and place 84
stereophonic sound 92, 93
Strachan, Barney 146–7
studio work 74–85, 169
  see also recording systems
surround sound systems 21, 91, 133, 136
synthesis 86–9, 96, 99
synthesisers 17, 26, 28, 88

tape recorders 16, 25
technology
  art relationship 13
  artists' use 49, 60–4
  developments 32–5
  historical perspective 14–18, 20–9
  media formats 148–51
  presenting work 110–11
  radio work 70
  see also computer technology; digital technology
'Triphonic Turntable' 54–5, 59–60
turntablism 122, 123

Varèse, Edgard 16, 30–1, 134–5
video sound 90–2
vinyl records 55, 60–1
vision 37, 55–61, 63
vocoders 80, 82–3

web streaming 71
websites 168–9
Welles, Orson 25

Credits

Acknowledgements

A book like this may have only one acknowledged author but, in truth, it stems from and is made possible by the efforts and contributions of many people: those who inspire by their works and especially those who give of their time and knowledge either directly or through providing information, making themselves available for chats and by acting as sounding boards for ideas. In a very real sense, this book is every bit as much theirs as it is mine.

Many people contributed in many ways to help make this book possible and I'm hugely grateful to every one of them. So, in no particular order, the biggest of all possible thank yous to:

My brilliant colleagues at Middlesex University: John Dack, Salomé Voegelin, Martin Robinson, Nic Sandiland, Nye Parry, Andrew Deakin, Matt Abrey and the late and much-missed Hugh Davies for many helpful suggestions and hours of inspiring and informative conversations; Stephen Boyd Davis and Huw Jones of the Lansdown Centre for Electronic Arts for support and encouragement; our outstanding students past and present (including Nathan Mann and Dani Joss to whom special thanks for pictures of their work); the management of Middlesex University who unwittingly made the whole project possible; our 'guest artists': Vicki Bennett, Max Eastley, Janek Schaefer, Simon Emmerson and Knut Aufermann for taking the time to talk about and provide pictures of their work; Hannah Gibbs for interview transcription; Humphrey and Ollie for workstation breaks and John and Sally Mitchell for invaluable hospitality.

Particular thanks to Karen Wilks for graphic design and layout and to Caroline Walmsley and Leafy Robinson, my editors at AVA, for guiding the whole project. Thanks also to Lucy Bryan, Sanaz Nazemi, Martin Blain and Amy Morgan.

Index compiled by INDEXING SPECIALISTS (UK) Ltd, Indexing House, 306A Portland Road, Hove, East Sussex BN3 5LP. Tel: 01273 416777. email: richardr@indexing.co.uk Website: www.indexing.co.uk

None of this would have been possible without the support and frequent forgiveness of the rest of the household especially my long-suffering wife Louise: this is for her with thanks and love.

Notes